# THE LAND WE LEFT BEHIND

### A pictorial history
### and memories
### of the war years in the South Hams

Produced to commemorate the
60th Anniversary of D-Day

Copyright ©
**Robin  Rose-Price**
and
**Jean  Parnell**

*In association with*
*The Blackawton and Strete History Group*

ORCHARD PUBLICATIONS
2  Orchard Close, Chudleigh, Devon TQ13 0LR
Telephone: (01626) 852714

ISBN 1898964610

*Printed by*
Hedgerow Print, Crediton, Devon EX17 1ES

# Contents

# Acknowledgements

A special thank you to the Blackawton and Strete History Group whose idea it was to produce a book to commemorate the 60th Anniversary of the D-Day landings on the Normandy coast on the 6th June 1944.

We would like to thank the Dartmouth Museum and the Cookworthy Museum in Kingsbridge, who gave their permission to use some of the pictures from their photographic archives, for this book.

Many local people should be mentioned for their encouragement and contributions and we would like to thank Angela and Paul Lansdale, Humphrey Waterhouse, Una Taster, Brian and Elizabeth Kingsley, John Hannaford, Brian Smalley, John Godfrey, Bill Ireland and Peggy Watkins. Ian Davidson kindly gave us permission to use Ted Archer's *Exercise Tiger* painting, page 48, and thanks to Ray Freeman for use of material from her book *We remember D-Day*.

A special thank you to Reg Hannaford, Basil Mitchelmore, Betty Tabb and Pam Wills whose great memories were a fund of information and for all their help in putting names to many of the photographs.

*For*
*my grandson*
*Euan Rose-Price*
*May he never have to experience the horrors of war*

# The Home Guard
## *Formed from the Local Defence Volunteers*
(nicknamed locally as Look, Drive and Vanish)

## Names of the C (*Start*) Company Home Guard 15th October 1944

**Back Row**
J.F.Edmonds   F.G.Shepard   W.F.Beer
W.H.Shepard   F.H.Farleigh   P.J.Hayman   S.N.Kelland   A.J.Farleigh   A.C.Johns   W.H.Elliott
J.T.Barberville   A.G.Trowt

**Row 6**
T.A.Wood   W.E.Tucker   -   A.P.Elliott   F.Thomas   R.G.Steer   E.Arundell   J.Reeds   W.F.Pack
R.T.Friend   L.C.Rogers

**Row 5**
L/Corpl G.E.Moore   Corpl.E.Lapthorn   W.P.Ball   Corpl. S.Hutchins   Corpl.R.Cater   Corpl.
W.E.Baskerville   Corpl. W.Powlesland   Corpl. L.A.Barry   Corpl. C.A.Jarvis   J.E.Parker

**Row 4**
R.E.Steer   E.E.Putt   C.H.Stone   C.Thomas   Sergt R.H.Johns   Sergt R.Leach   Sergt C.W.Mitchelmore
Sergt W.J.Sanders   Sergt F. Osborne   Sergt L.A.Clayton

**Row 3**
Sergt S.Favis   Sergt J.E.Hannaford   Sergt P.Tabb   Miss L.Luckes   Miss M.Wakeham   Miss B.Arundell
Lt H.Ford   Lt T.H.Brooking   Lt S.E.Hockridge   Capt. C.W.Clarke   Major A.H. Arundell

**Row 2**
G.T.Edmunds   J.E.Wotton   A.H.Luckes   E.H.Luckes   W.H.Beer   W.G.Wakeham   S.R.Roper
N.R.Johns   R.S.Johns   W.G.Stone

**Front Row**
T.W.Tucker   R.V.Tucker   J.S.Mitchelmore   A.W.French   J.L.Elliott   C.Johns   A.G.Helmer
T.R.Helmer   W.F.Johns

## Present 131  Total strength 208

**Back Row**  G.E.Stumbles  A.E.Corner
J.E.Stone  W.J.Ball  A.Winzer  S.S.Putt  S.E.Luscombe      H.P.Stumbles  G.Butt
**Row 6**
N.M.Bois  F.Taylor  W.A.Partridge  R.C.Luscombe  R.L.Stone  J.R.Putt  A.G.Tabb
**Row 5**
Corpl. W.A.Pike  Corpl. E.G.Morriss  Corpl. P.Marshmam  Corpl. H.E.Rogers  Corpl. L.E.Luscombe
Corpl V.R.Rogers  H.C.Coursens  L/Corpl. E.B.Lethbridge
**Row 4**
Sergt. W.H.Stone    Sergt. R.L.Piper    Sergt. H.A.Luscombe  Sergt.H.A.Jamieson    Sergt. W.J.
Caunter  W.G.Hatcher  W.C.Wright  P.N.Tolchard  C.J.Rogers
**Row 3**
Lt. C.M.Cruckshank  Lt. C.W.Halse  Lt. R.R.Foale  Lt. R.C.Tyler  C.S.M.  A.H. Mitchelmore
C.S.M.  A.S.Purdy  Mrs. H.Stumbles  Mrs. S.E.Luscombe  Sergt. W.G.Stone  Sergt.C.A.Stone
G.E.Rundle
**Row 2**
F.M.Chase   S.A.Shepherd   G.E.Stone   W.J.Olver   M.L.Rendle   F.E.Hutchings   R.J.Putt
H.H.Hannaford
**Front Row**
R.Hender  H. Hutchings  J.F.Shepard  R.E.Wills  J. Fey    W.H.Lamble   J.F.Blank

3

# Women played an important part in the war

The Land Army attracted many girls from the cities who came down to work on the farms to help feed Britain.

The WVS fulfilled many different roles including supplying meals for the home guard as pictured.

The Wrens - seen here in charge of the picket boats in Dartmouth Harbour. Their duties 'freed a man for the fleet'.

A group of Wrens on a balcony overlooking the River Dart, now the building occupied by the restaurant 'Piz zazz'.

Nurses – tended the sick and wounded. Seen here outside Combe Royal in Kingsbridge

Mary Rogers *(late of the Torcross Hotel)* was a driver for the S.O.E

Mary was one of the drivers who transported secret agents from their safe houses to their point of departure for overseas assignments. One of these agents, she drove regularly, was code named 'White Rabbit'. She also drove the 'top brass' around London from her base at S.O.E headquarters in Baker Street, and when required she took them to Bletchley for secret meetings.

Mary drove down to Slapton Sands with some senior officers who were observing 'Exercise Tiger'.

# 1940.  Early war damage

On the 27th November 1940 a bomb dropped in the yard behind Harwood's Shop on Torcross sea front. The explosion flattened the buildings around it. The Harwood family escaped without serious injury. It is said that the thatched roof remained intact when the walls collapsed and fell like a huge tea-cosy over the people below, showering them with dust and spiders, but saving their lives.

A pile of rubble is all that remains of Harwood's Shop.  Waterside house was built on the site in 1951.

In 1942 another bomb was dropped from low level in the dark and landed on the hillside above Torcross village. The back-blast lifted all the slates off the roofs around the square and Hannaford's yard. Margaret Hannaford is checking to see if her car has been damaged.

Even nature seemed determined to create havoc! The original barbed wire defence in front of Torcross was destroyed by a violent easterly storm. It was replaced with a much higher structure.

# Life carried on

Although barbed wire defences were erected in front of Torcross village, small gaps were left so that the local families could still use the beach. Margaret and Una Hannaford with Marion Colliver from the Torcross shop and cafe.

Elizabeth Kingsley (nee Colton) and her brothers John and Robert, playing in front of Port Cottage, where they stayed with their grandparents – Mr and Mrs Latham.

# 4th November 1943.    We were told to leave

The chairman of the Devon County Council, Sir John Daw, was ordered to requisition an area of 30,000 acres as shown on the map below. This included the villages of Torcross, Stokenham, Chillington, Blackawton, East Allington, Slapton, Strete, Frogmore and Sherford. It also included 180 farms and many small hamlets. It affected 750 families and totalled 3000 men, women and children

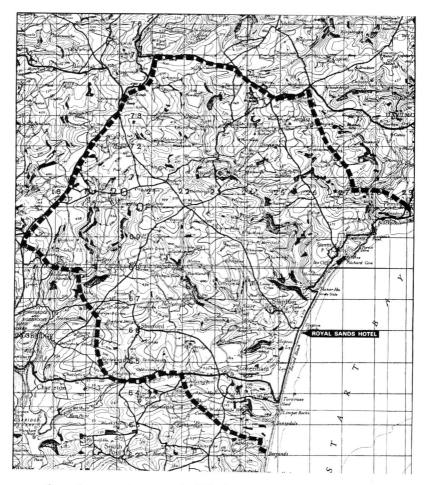

The area was from the sea at the east end of Blackpool Bay in the parish of Stoke Fleming, along the Hemborough Post road to Hemborough Post.   Then along the Dittisham – Halwell Road from Hemborough Post to the cross-road a quarter of a mile east of the village of Halwell. From this cross-road along the Kingsbridge Road to the Woodleigh / Buckland cross-roads. Thence along the road to Buckland – Frogmore – Chillington and to the sea at Beesands (but excluding the village of Beesands).

## 12th November 1943

Notices having been posted, the first public meeting was held at East Allington. The following day further meetings were held at Blackawton and Slapton. People were ordered to leave their houses and farms which in some cases families had occupied for many generations, taking with them all their possessions including farm animals and pets.

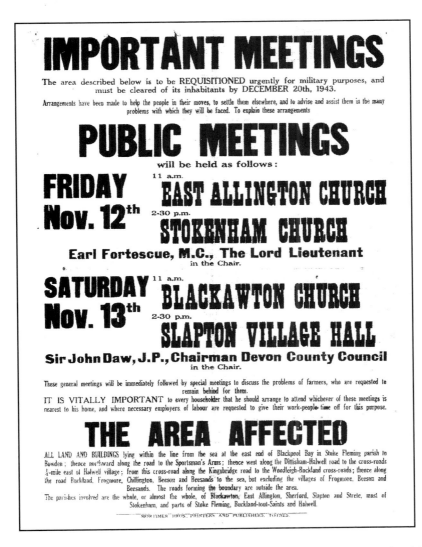

There was very little protest as it was war time, but it was very difficult for the elderly to understand, especially the farmers who had to leave crops in the ground knowing that there was a desperate shortage of food in Britain.

**Notice sent to every house in the area**

THIS GIVES YOU IMPORTANT INFORMATION AND ADVICE. PLEASE READ IT CAREFULLY

**FIRST OF ALL** fill in as fully as you can the enquiry form you will find with these papers. There is a space provided for your special problems; use it, and write on the back if you have not room in front. A W.V.S. representative will come to collect the form after 4 days, and will, if you ask her help you to, fill it in. If you come to the Information Centre before the form has been collected, bring it with you.

**INFORMATION CENTRES** will be set up at Stokenham (for the Parishes of Stokenham, Slapton, Sherford and Buckland Tout Saints) and at Blackawton (for the Parishes of Blackawton, East Allington, Woodleigh, Halwell, Stoke Fleming and Strete). They will be open daily from 9.30.am. to 6.00 p.m. You will find their officers, who will be able to advise and help you, whatever the difficulty may be. Do not hesitate to make the fullest use of your Centre. Take your little worries there, as well as your big ones. But you must go to the Centre to which the Parish in which you live has been allotted. Whether you are going to move yourself, or whether you are looking for us to move you, fix as early a date for your departure as you can. Of course you would like to stay in your home until the last possible day. But those who go first are going to get the best accommodation and the best transport, so don't wait for the rush, the hurry and the discomfort of the last few days.

**HOW YOU CAN BE HELPED**

**1. COMPENSATION**
On all questions concerning compensation about which you are not clear you should consult the Admiralty. They have offices at both Information Centres, and wherever possible an Officer will visit you and give you any explanations you require.

**2. ACCOMMODATION**
You should endeavor at once to find other accommodation for yourself and family outside the area (of which the boundaries are given at the end of this note). If you find it impossible to make your own arrangements in this way, the Local Authorities will find you accommodation outside the area, but they can give no guarantee of an unfurnished house or rooms and it is almost certain that compulsory billeting in an occupied house will be necessary. If you have special difficulties due to your being unable to find accommodation suitable for invalids, expectant mothers, old and infirm people, you should say so when filling in your form and should consult the Information Centre as well.

## BILLETING

If you are provided with accommodation for yourself and family in an occupied house, whether by your own arrangement or by the authorities, the householder will be entitled to a billeting allowance at the rate of 5/- per week for each adult and 3/- per week for each child under the age of 14. This billeting allowance will be payable for TWO WEEKS without recovery but if the payment of the allowance is continued beyond two weeks, recovery will be made from you up to the full amount of the allowance, according to your financial circumstances.

If you are making your own arrangements to share accommodation with relatives, friends or other family outside the area, you should apply to the Information Centre for the issue of a certificate authorizing the payment of billeting allowances.

## 3. TRANSPORT

The reasonable cost of all necessary journeys will be paid to you, and owners of vehicles of any kind may use them freely for the removal from the area of their families, furniture and effects or those of their neighbours. If you have a motor vehicle which is unlicensed, you can obtain from the Information Centre a special certificate which will enable you to use it for the above purposes within an area and for a period which will be entered in the certificate. You may also use your private car to go to the Information Centre, or to make reasonable journeys outside the area in connection with accommodation, storage or employment.

In all these cases you can obtain petrol coupons from the Information Centre. Cars can also be made available by the Information Centre to take you on necessary journeys.

During the first fortnight you will be able to make your own arrangements for the removal of your furniture with a furniture remover or other carrier (of which the reasonable cost will be repaid you). In this way you will be able to arrange your move to suit your own convenience.

After this fortnight all transport is likely to be controlled, and will then only be obtainable through the Information Centres. All applications to the Centres should give full details of the time and place at which the transport is required, the load (e.g. contents of a four-roomed cottage) and the destination. Transport will then be provided according to a planned programme designed to secure speed and economy.

## 4. STORAGE

If you are going to store your furniture you should make arrangements with a repository outside the area. If you cannot find storage room there, come to the Information Centre, and arrangements will be made for you.

## 5. FARMERS

Every help will be given you by the War Agricultural Executive Committee at Blackawton including assistance in the removal or disposal of your stock and of your cattle food and other farm produce, and in making arrangements to enable you to complete your threshing and lifting your roots.

## 6. FARM WORKERS

If you work on a farm, or do any other work actually connected with farming at Blackawton, you should consult the representative of the War Agricultural Executive Committee who will find you work. You should not go in search of work yourself, but if you do find a new farm post of your own you should tell the War Agricultural Executive Committee at once.

## 7. OTHER PERSONS SEEKING EMPLOYMENT

Should consult the representative of the Ministry of Labour at the Information Centre.

## 8. SHOPKEEPERS

A representative of the Ministry of Food or the Board of Trade will visit you as soon as possible, and will make arrangements for the removal and disposal of your stocks. If you keep a food shop, and wish to move at an early date (i.e. before your customers have gone) you should at once inform the Food Executive Officer, Kingsbridge Rural District, of your intention.

## 9. RATION BOOKS AND IDENTITY CARDS

As you will be changing your address it will be necessary in due course to amend the particulars on your ration book and identity card. You should enquire at your local food office or at your Information Centre how you should proceed.

## 10. PUBLICANS

Your Licensee will not be extinguished by the closing of your houses.   It will come into force again on your return.

## 11. EDUCATION

Elementary school children will attend school at the places to which they move.

The parents of children attending secondary schools should inform the Information Centre. Individual arrangements will be made to enable them to continue their studies.

## 12. PENSIONS AND ASSISTANCE

Give in your form particulars of pensions or any form of monetary aid received by any member of your household.  Representatives of the Assistance Board will visit all persons in receipt of supplementary pensions, and will deal with any case in which urgent financial assistance is required.  Arrangements will be made for the prompt payment of Old Age Pensions at the post office of the place to which the pensioner has transferred.

### 13. POST OFFICE SERVICES

The post office will make arrangements for the prompt forwarding of letters, and will deliver at your house a re-direction card to be filled up. At the same time, you should be careful to notify your change of address to member of your family especially to those who are serving in the Forces.

### 14. PROFITEERING

Any attempt to charge you unfair rent, or to profiteer on transport or storage charges, should be reported at once to the Information Centre, and, in the case of rent, to the Local Authority concerned.

### THE AREA OUTSIDE WHICH YOU MUST SEEK NEW ACCOMMODATION

From the sea at the east end of Blackpool Bay in Stoke Fleming parish, along the Hemborough Post road to Hemborough Post. Then along the Dittisham-Halwell road from Hemborough Post to the crossroad a quarter of a mile east of Halwell village. From this crossroad along the Kingsbridge road to the Woodleigh-Buckland cross roads. Thence along the road Buckland-Frogmore-Woodleigh-Buckland crossroads. Thence along the road Buckland-Frogmore-Chillington and to the sea at Beesands (but excluding the village of Beesands).

The parishes involved are the whole, or almost the whole of Blackawton, East Allington, Sherford, Slapton and Strete and a part of the parishes of Stoke Fleming, Buckland tout Saints, Stokenham, Woodleigh and Halwell.

# December 1943. The Americans arrive

Much discussion took place about the evacuation at the King's Arms at Strete. Behind the bar are the landlord, Alf Britnell and his wife and Fred Horton. Amongst those on the other side of the bar are Mr.Goodman and Nat Veasey.

The GIs share a final drink with some of the locals at the Queens Arms at Slapton before the pub is closed for the duration. Vera Lavers (the landlady), Herman Trowt, Tom Dick Tabb (with the cap), Bert Trowt. The American GIs are Corpl. Le Blanc and Private Coan.

The arrival of the Americans is overseen by Constable Roy Betts.

At the beginning of December the first GIs arrive outside 'The Chantry' which was to become their billet and mess hall. They were here to help the residents pack up their belongings.

The Americans quickly make friends with Basil Mitchelmore, Mike Bowles and Terrance Rogers, by sharing out candy and chewing gum.

The three friends cannot believe their luck. Sweets had been virtually non-existent until now because of food rationing.

Valerie and Marlene Tabb and Roy Bullen wait hopefully for some candy that their friends had received. Roy Bullen's mother and baby brother were both killed when a bomb was dropped on Beesands.

Marjorie Roper is talking to constable Betts who is keeping a watchful eye on the newcomers.

# Field Kitchens

Miss K. Goldsmith and Mr Mudd preparing a meal in a communal kitchen in Strete for all the remaining residents whose own kitchens had already been taken to the various destinations of the individual families.

Catering for large numbers always generates a lot of big pots to be washed.

Basil Mitchelmore and Milwyn Mitchelmore (not related) watch a G I boiling water in the grounds of the 'Chantry'. This was the only hot water available for the soldiers needs.

Packing cases and boxes were provided by the authorities as Fred Blank and his daughter in law, Kathleen (nee Buckingham), start to move out their furniture.

# Every form of transport was used for the evacuation

Fred Blank is talking to an American truck driver. Milwyn Mitchelmore is looking over the wall. Army vehicles were used fully to help with the evacuation.

Edward Hannaford helps Frank Rogers remove his equipment from the butcher's shop in Slapton with the help of Bert Trout. Pearl Mitchelmore (nee Rogers) looks on. The equipment was taken out to Prawle where the Hannafords set up their butcher's shop.

Every type of transport available was used to move the villagers' belongings as the residents of Blackawton moved out. Special petrol coupons were made available so that vehicles could make as many return journeys as necessary to empty the houses.

Alan and Bernard Fardon, whose father was the blacksmith in Blackawton, help out with a wheelbarrow.

Russell Lucas is collecting the last few items from a house in the narrows at Chillington. All the houses were locked up as the owners left and they were told that no one would go into them. However many of them were used and left in poor condition.

# Farms also had to be cleared

Hay-ricks were protected with thatch, in the hope that they would survive until the farmers were able to return to their farms. Root crops had to be dug up and many other tasks were carried out.

Arthur Jarvis is taking his steam tractor and his threshing machine to a location outside the restricted area.

Livestock was moved onto farms outside the evacuated area, or sold at special auctions in Totnes and Kingsbridge. Sadly because so many were for sale at the same time, they fetched very low prices.

Land cleared ready to build the construction of the army camps and for the arrival of military equipment. The first GIs to arrive were drafted in to build these camps. Many of them were of African descent. It was the first time many of the locals had encountered a black person.

# Protection of the churches

The Admiralty informed the church commissioners that the safety of the church valuables could not be guaranteed.  So all carved screens, pulpits and fonts were taken down and carefully packed away, along with any other artefacts.

The font and other priceless religious relics are carefully packed away.

GIs help with the safe packing of the very delicate rood screen. Many of these screens had been in place for so many years that many of the parts were riddled with woodworm and in extremely fragile condition.

Mr Shepard the carpenter helping to take down the screen in Slapton Church. The home guard and the GIs help with the sandbags to protect the church from bombardment. These are placed around the items that could not be moved and in front of the stained glass window at the foot of the belfry.

Notice left on the door of each church

## To our Allies from the U.S.A.

This church has stood here for several hundred years. Around it has grown a community which have lived in these houses and tilled the fields ever since there was a church.

This church, this churchyard in which their loved ones lie at rest, these homes, these fields are as dear to those who have left them as are the homes and graves and fields which you, our allies have left behind you. They hope to return one day, as you hope to return to yours, to find them waiting to welcome them home. They entrust them to your care meanwhile and pray that God's blessing rest upon us all.

Charles, Bishop of Exeter

## The American Forces are told how to behave

This book was found in the rafters of the house belonging to Paul and Angela Lansdale who live in Torcross. It was issued to every American soldier. It tells them how they are expected to behave whilst stationed in the UK

*By kind permission of Paul and Angela Lansdale*

29

## INTRODUCTION

YOU are going to Great Britain as part of an Allied offensive—to meet Hitler and beat him on his own ground. For the time being you will be Britain's guest. The purpose of this guide is to start getting you acquainted with the British, their country, and their ways.

America and Britain are allies. Hitler knows that they are both powerful countries, tough and resourceful. He knows that they, with the other United Nations, mean his crushing defeat in the end.

So it is only common sense to understand that the first and major duty Hitler has given his propaganda chiefs is to separate Britain and America and spread distrust between them. If he can do that, his chance of winning *might* return.

**No Time To Fight Old Wars.** If you come from an Irish-American family, you may think of the English as persecutors of the Irish, or you may think of them as enemy Redcoats who fought against us in the American Revolution and the War of 1812. But there is no time today to fight old wars over again or bring up old grievances. We don't worry about which side our grandfathers fought on in the Civil War, because it doesn't mean anything now.

We can defeat Hitler's propaganda with a weapon of our own. Plain, common horse sense; understanding of evident truths.

The most evident truth of all is that in their major ways of life the British and American people are much alike. They speak the same language. They both believe in representative government, in freedom of worship, in freedom of speech. But each country has minor national characteristics which differ. It is by causing misunderstanding over these minor differences that Hitler hopes to make his propaganda effective.

**British Reserved, Not Unfriendly.** You defeat enemy propaganda not by denying that these differences exist, but by admitting them openly and then trying to understand them. For instance: The British are often more reserved in conduct than we. On a small crowded island where forty-five million people live, each man learns to guard his privacy carefully—and is equally careful not to invade another man's privacy.

So if Britons sit in trains or busses without striking up conversation with you, it doesn't mean they are being haughty and unfriendly. Probably they are paying more attention to you than you think. But they don't speak to you because they don't want to appear intrusive or rude.

Another difference. The British have phrases and colloquialisms of their own that may sound funny to you. You can make just as many boners in their eyes. It isn't a good idea, for instance, to say "bloody" in mixed company in Britain—it is one of their worst swear words. To say: "I look like a bum" is offensive to their ears, for to the British this means that you look like your own backside. It isn't important—just a tip if you are trying to shine in polite society. Near the end of this guide you will find more of these differences of speech.

British money is in pounds, shillings, and pence. (This also is explained more fully later on.) The British are used to this system and they like it, and all your arguments that the American decimal system is better won't convince them. They won't be pleased to hear you call it "funny money," either. They sweat hard to get it (wages are much lower in Britain than America) and they won't think you smart or funny for mocking at it.

**Don't Be a Show Off.** The British dislike bragging and showing off. American wages and American soldier's pay are the highest in the world. When pay day comes, it would be sound practice to learn to spend your money according to British standards. They consider

haughty and unfriendly. Probably they are paying more attention to you than you think. But they don't speak to you because they don't want to appear intrusive or rude.

Another difference. The British have phrases and colloquialisms of their own that may sound funny to you. You can make just as many boners in their eyes. It isn't a good idea, for instance, to say "bloody" in mixed company in Britain—it is one of their worst swear words. To say: "I look like a bum" is offensive to their ears, for to the British this means that you look like your own backside. It isn't important—just a tip if you are trying to shine in polite society. Near the end of this guide you will find more of these differences of speech.

British money is in pounds, shillings, and pence. (This also is explained more fully later on.) The British are used to this system and they like it, and all your arguments that the American decimal system is better won't convince them. They won't be pleased to hear you call it "funny money," either. They sweat hard to get it (wages are much lower in Britain than America) and they won't think you smart or funny for mocking at it.

**Don't Be a Show Off.** The British dislike bragging and showing off. American wages and American soldier's pay are the highest in the world. When pay day comes, it would be sound practice to learn to spend your money according to British standards. They consider

you highly paid. They won't think any better of you for throwing money around; they are more likely to feel that you haven't learned the common-sense virtues of thrift. The British "Tommy" is apt to be specially touchy about the difference between his wages and yours. Keep this in mind. Use common sense and don't rub him the wrong way.

You will find many things in Britain physically different from similar things in America. But there are also important similarities—our common speech, our common law, and our ideals of religious freedom were all brought from Britain when the Pilgrims landed at Plymouth Rock. Our ideas about political liberties are also British and parts of our own Bill of Rights were borrowed from the great charters of British liberty.

Remember that in America you like people to conduct themselves as we do, and to respect the same things. Try to do the same for the British and respect the things they treasure.

**The British Are Tough.**  Don't be misled by the British tendency to be soft-spoken and polite. If they need to be, they can be plenty tough. The English language didn't spread across the oceans and over the mountains and jungles and swamps of the world because these people were panty-waists.

Sixty thousand British civilians—men, women, and children—have died under bombs, and yet the morale of British is unbreakable and high. A nation doesn't come through that, if it doesn't have plain, common guts. The British are tough, strong people, and good allies.

You won't be able to tell the British much about "taking it." They are not particularly interested in taking it any more. They are far more interested in getting together in solid friendship with us, so that we can all start dishing it out to Hitler.

### THE COUNTRY

YOU will find out right away that England is a small country, smaller than North Carolina or Iowa. The whole of Great Britain—that is England and Scotland and Wales together—is hardly bigger than Minnesota.

England's largest river, the Thames (pronounced "Tems") is not even as big as the Mississippi when it leaves Minnesota. No part of England is more than one hundred miles from the Sea.

If you are from Boston or Seattle the weather may remind you of home. If you are from Arizona or North Dakota you will find it a little hard to get used to. At first you will probably not like the almost continual rains and mists and the absence of snow and crisp cold. Actually, the city of London has less rain for the whole year than many places in the United States, but the rain falls in frequent drizzles. Most people get used to the English climate eventually.

If you have a chance to travel about you will agree that no area of the same size in the United States has such a variety of scenery. At one end of the English channel there is a coast like that of Maine. At the other end are the great white chalk cliffs of Dover. The lands of South England and the Thames Valley are like farm or grazing lands of the eastern United States, while the lake country in the north of England and the highlands of Scotland are like the White Mountains of New Hampshire. In the east, where England bulges out toward Holland, the land is almost Dutch in appearance, low, flat, and marshy. The great wild moors of Yorkshire in the north and Devon in the southwest will remind you of the Badlands of Dakota and Montana.

**Age Instead of Size.** On furlough you will probably go to the cities, where you will meet the Briton's pride in age and tradition. You will find that the British care little about size, not having the "biggest" of many things as we do. For instance, London has no skyscrapers. Not because English architects couldn't design one, but because London is built on swampy ground, not on a rock like New York, and skyscrapers need something solid to rest their foundations on. In London they will point out to you buildings like Westminster Abbey, where England's kings and greatest men are buried, and St. Paul's Cathedral with its famous dome, and the Tower of London, which was built almost a thousand years ago. All of these buildings have played an important part in England's history. They mean just as much to the British as Mount Vernon or Lincoln's birthplace do to us.

The largest English cities are all located in the lowlands near the various seacoasts. (See the map in the center of this guide.) In the southeast, on the Thames, is London—which is the combined New York, Washington, and Chicago not only of England but of the far-flung British Empire. Greater London's huge population of twelve million people is the size of Greater New York City and all its suburbs with the nearby New Jersey cities thrown in. It is also more than a quarter of the total population of the British Isles. The great "midland" manufacturing cities of Birmingham, Sheffield, and Coventry (sometimes called "the Detroit of Britain") are located in the central part of England. Nearby on the west coast are the textile and shipping centers of Manchester and Liverpool. Further north, in Scotland, is the world's leading ship-building center of Glasgow. On the east side of Scotland is the historic Scottish capital, Edinburgh, scene of the tales of Scott and Robert Louis Stevenson which many of you read in school. In southwest England at the broad mouth of the Severn is the great port of Bristol.

**Remember There's a War On.** Britain may look a little shop-worn and grimy to you. The British people are anxious to have you know that you are not seeing their country at its best. There's been a war on since 1939. The houses haven't been painted because factories are not making paint—they're making planes. The famous English gardens and parks are either unkept because there are no men to take care of them, or they are being used to grow needed vegetables. British taxicabs look antique because Britain makes tanks for herself and Russia and hasn't time to make new cars. British trains are cold because power is needed for industry, not for heating. There are no luxury dining cars on trains because total war effort has no place for such frills. The trains are unwashed and grimy because men and women are needed for more important work than car-washing. The British people are anxious for you to know that in normal times Britain looks much prettier, cleaner, neater.

### GOVERNMENT

ALTHOUGH you'll read in the papers about "lords" and "sirs," England is still one of the great democracies and the cradle of many American liberties. Personal rule by the King has been dead in England for nearly a thousand years. Today the King reigns, but does not govern. The British people have great affection for their monarch but they have stripped him of practically all political power. It is well to remember this in your comings and goings about England. Be careful not to criticize the King. The British feel about that the way you would feel if anyone spoke against our country or our flag. Today's King and Queen stuck with the people through the blitzes and had their home bombed just like anyone else, and the people are proud of them.

**Britain the Cradle of Democracy.** Today the old power of the King has been shifted to Parliament, the Prime Minister, and his Cabinet. The British Parliament has been called the mother of parliaments, because almost all the representative bodies in the world have been copied from it. It is made up of two houses, the House of Commons and the House of Lords. The House of Commons is the most powerful group and is elected by all adult men and women in the country, much like our Congress. Today the House of Lords can do little more than add its approval to laws passed by the House of Commons. Many of the "titles" held by the lords (such as "baron" and "duke" and "earl") have been passed from father to son for hundreds of years. Others are granted in reward for outstanding achievement, much as American colleges and universities give honorary degrees to famous men and women. These customs may seem strange and old-fashioned but they give the British the same feeling of security and comfort that many of us get from the familiar ritual of a church service.

The important thing to remember is that within this apparently old-fashioned framework the British enjoy a practical, working twentieth century democracy which is in some ways even more flexible and sensitive to the will of the people than our own.

### THE PEOPLE—THEIR CUSTOMS AND MANNERS

THE BEST WAY to get on in Britain is very much the same as the best way to get on in America. The same sort of courtesy and decency and friendliness that go over big in America will go over big in Britain. The British have seen a good many Americans and they like Americans. They will like your frankness as long as it is friendly. They will expect you to be generous. They are not given to back-slapping and they are shy about showing their affections. But once they get to like you they make the best friends in the world.

In "getting along" the first important thing to remember is that the British are like the Americans in many ways—but not in *all* ways. You will quickly discover differences that seem confusing and even wrong. Like driving on the left side of the road, and having money based on an "impossible" accounting system, and drinking warm beer. But once you get used to things like that, you will realize that they belong to England just as baseball and jazz and coca-cola belong to us.

**The British Like Sports.** The British of all classes are enthusiastic about sports, both as amateurs and as spectators of professional sports. They love to shoot, they love to play games, they ride horses and bet on horse races, they fish. (But be careful where you hunt or fish. Fishing and hunting rights are often private property.)

The great "spectator" sports are football in the autumn and winter and cricket in the spring and summer. See a "match" in either of these sports whenever you get a chance. You will get a kick out of it—if only for the differences from American sports.

Cricket will strike you as slow compared with American baseball, but it isn't easy to play well. You will probably get more fun out of "village cricket" which corresponds to sandlot baseball than you would out of one of the big three-day professional matches. The big professional matches are often nothing but a private contest between the bowler (who corresponds to our pitcher) and the batsman (batter) and you have to know the fine points of the game to understand what is going on.

Football in Britain takes two forms. They play soccer, which is known in America; and they also play "rugger," which is a rougher game and closer to American football, but is played without the padded suits and headguards we use. Rugger requires fifteen on a side, uses a ball slightly bigger than our football, and allows lateral but not forward passing. The English do not handle the ball as cleanly as we do, but they are far more expert with their feet. As in all English games, no substitutes are allowed. If a man is injured, his side continues with fourteen players and so on.

You will find that English crowds at football or cricket matches are more orderly and more polite to the players than American crowds. If a fielder misses a catch at cricket, the crowd will probably take a sympathetic attitude. They will shout "good try" even if it looks to you like a bad fumble. In America the crowd would probably shout "take him out." This contrast should be remembered. It means that you must be careful in the excitement of an English game not to shout out remarks which everyone in America would understand, but which the British might think insulting.

In general more people play games in Britain than in America and they play the game even if they are not good at it. You can always find people who play no better than you and are glad to play with you. They are good sportsmen and are quick to recognize good sportsmanship wherever they meet it.

**Indoor Amusements.** The British have theaters and movies (which they call "cinemas") as we do. But the great place of recreation is the "pub." A pub, or public house, is what we could call a bar or tavern. The usual drink is beer, which is not an imitation of German beer as our beer is, but ale. (But they usually call it beer or "bitter.") Not much whiskey is now being drunk. Wartime taxes have shot the price of a bottle up to about $4.50. The British are beer-drinkers—and can hold it. The beer is now below peacetime strength, but can still make a man's tongue wag at both ends.

You will be welcome in the British pubs as long as you remember one thing. The pub is "the poor man's club," the neighborhood or village gathering place, where the men have come to see their friends, not strangers. If you want to join a darts game, let them ask you first (as they probably will). And if you are beaten it is the custom to stand aside and let someone else play.

The British make much of Sunday. All the shops are closed, most of the restaurants are closed, and in the small towns there is not much to do. You had better follow the example of the British and try to spend Sunday afternoon in the country.

British churches, particularly the little village churches, are often very beautiful inside and out. Most of them are always open and if you feel like it, do not hesitate to walk in. But do not walk around if a service is going on.

You will naturally be interested in getting to know your opposite number, the British soldier, the "Tommy" you have heard and read about. You can understand that two actions on your part will slow up the friendship—swiping his girl, and not appreciating what his army has been up against. Yes, and rubbing it in that you are better paid than he is.

Children the world over are easy to get along with. British children are much like our own. The British have reserved much of the food that gets through solely for their children. To the British children you as an American

will be "something special." For they have been fed at their schools and impressed with the fact that the food they ate was sent to them by Uncle Sam. You don't have to tell the British about lend-lease food. They know about it and appreciate it.

**Keep Out of Arguments.** You can rub a Britisher the wrong way by telling him "we came over and won the last one." Each nation did its share. But Britain remembers that nearly a million of her best manhood died in the last war. America lost 60,000 in action.

Such arguments and the war debts along with them are dead issues. Nazi propaganda now is pounding away day and night asking the British people why they should fight "to save Uncle Shylock and his silver dollar." Don't play into Hitler's hands by mentioning war debts.

Neither do the British need to be told that their armies lost the first couple of rounds in the present war. We've lost a couple, ourselves, so do not start off by being critical of them and saying what the Yanks are going to do. Use your head before you sound off, and remember how long the British alone held Hitler off without any help from anyone.

In the pubs you will hear a lot of Britons openly criticizing their government and the conduct of the war. That isn't an occasion for you to put in your two-cents worth. It's their business, not yours. You sometimes criticize members of your own family—but just let an outsider start doing the same, and you know how you feel!

The Briton is just as outspoken and independent as we are. But don't get him wrong. He is also the most law-abiding citizen in the world, because the British system of justice is just about the best there is. There are fewer murders, robberies, and burglaries in the whole of Great Britain in a year than in a single large American city.

Once again, look, listen, and learn before you start telling the British how much better we do things. They will be interested to hear about life in America and you have a great chance to overcome the picture many of them have gotten from the movies of an America made up of wild Indians and gangsters. When you find differences between British and American ways of doing things, there is usually a good reason for them.

British railways have dinky freight cars (which they call "goods wagons") not because they don't know any better. Small cars allow quicker handling of freight at the thousands and thousands of small stations.

British automobiles are little and low-powered. That's because all the gasoline has to be imported over thousands of miles of ocean.

British taxicabs have comic-looking front wheel structures. Watch them turn around in a 12-foot street and you'll understand why.

The British don't know how to make a good cup of coffee. You don't know how to make a good cup of tea. It's an even swap.

The British are leisurely—but not really slow. Their crack trains held world speed records. A British ship held the trans-Atlantic record. A British car and a British driver set world's speed records in America.

Do not be offended if Britishers do not pay as full respects to national or regimental colors as Americans do. The British do not treat the flag as such an important

symbol as we do. But they pay more frequent respect to their national anthem. In peace or war "God Save the King" (to the same tune of our "America") is played at the conclusion of all public gatherings such as theater performances. The British consider it bad form not to stand at attention, even if it means missing the last bus. If you are in a hurry, leave *before* the national anthem is played. That's considered alright.

On the whole, British people—whether English, Scottish, or Welsh—are open and honest. If you are on furlough and puzzled about directions, money, or customs, most people will be anxious to help you as long as you speak first and without bluster. The best authority on all problems is the nearest "bobby" (policeman) in his steel helmet. British police are proud of being able to answer almost any question under the sun. They're not in a hurry and they'll take plenty of time to talk to you.

*The British will welcome you as friends and allies.* But remember that crossing the ocean doesn't automatically make you a hero. There are housewives in aprons and youngsters in knee pants in Britain who have lived through more high explosives in air raids than many soldiers saw in first class barrages in the last war.

### BRITAIN AT WAR

AT HOME in America you were in a country at war. Since your ship left port, however, you have been in a *war zone*. You will find that all Britain is a war zone and has been since September 1939. All this has meant great changes in the British way of life.

Every light in England is blacked out every night and all night. Every highway signpost has come down and barrage balloons have gone up. Grazing land is now ploughed for wheat and flower beds turned into vegetable gardens. Britain's peacetime army of a couple of hundred thousand has been expanded to over two million men. Everything from the biggest factory to the smallest village workshop is turning out something for the war, so that Britain can supply arms for herself, for Libya, India, Russia, and every front. Hundreds of thousands of women have gone to work in factories or joined the many military auxiliary forces. Old-time social distinctions are being forgotten as the sons of factory workers rise to be officers in the forces and the daughters of noblemen get jobs in munitions factories.

But more important than this is the effect of the war itself. The British have been bombed, night after night and month after month. Thousands of them have lost their houses, their possessions, their families. Gasoline, clothes, and railroad travel are hard to come by and incomes are cut by taxes to an extent we Americans have not even approached. One of the things the English always had enough of in the past was soap. Now it is so scarce that girls working in the factories often cannot get the grease off their hands or out of their hair. And food is more strictly rationed than anything else.

**The British Came Through.** For many months the people of Britain have been doing without things which Americans take for granted. But you will find that shortages, discomforts, blackouts, and bombings have not made the British depressed. They have a new cheerfulness and a new determination born out of hard times and tough luck. After going through what they have been through it's only human nature that they should be more than ever determined to win.

You are coming to Britain from a country where your home is still safe, food is still plentiful, and lights are still burning. So it is doubly important for you to remember that the British soldiers and civilians have been living under a tremendous strain. It is always impolite to criticize your hosts. It is militarily stupid to insult your allies. So stop and think before you sound off about lukewarm beer, or cold boiled potatoes, or the way English cigarettes taste.

If British civilians look dowdy and badly dressed, it is not because they do not like good clothes or know how to wear them. All clothing is rationed and the British know that they help war production by wearing an old suit or dress until it cannot be patched any longer. Old clothes are "good form."

One thing to be careful about—if you are invited into a British home and the host exhorts you to "eat up—there's plenty on the table," go easy. It may be the family's rations for a whole week spread out to show their hospitality.

**Waste Means Lives.** It is always said that Americans throw more food into their garbage cans than any other country eats. It is true. We have always been a "producer" nation. Most British food is imported even in peacetimes, and for the last two years the British have been taught not to waste the things that their ships bring in from abroad. British seamen die getting those convoys through. The British have been taught this so thoroughly that they now know that gasoline and food represent the lives of merchant sailors. And when you burn gasoline needlessly, it will seem to them as if you are wasting the blood of those seamen—when you destroy or waste food you have wasted the life of another sailor.

**British Women At War.** A British woman officer or non-commissioned officer can—and often does—give orders to a man private. The men obey smartly and know it is no shame. For British women have proven themselves in this war. They have stuck to their posts near burning ammunition dumps, delivered messages afoot after their motorcycles have been blasted from under them. They have pulled aviators from burning planes. They have died at the gun posts and as they fell another girl has stepped directly into the position and "carried on." There is not a *single record* in this war of any British woman in uniformed service quitting her post or failing in her duty under fire.

Now you understand why British soldiers respect the women in uniform. They have won the right to the utmost respect. When you see a girl in khaki or air-force blue with a bit of ribbon on her tunic—remember she didn't get it for knitting more socks than anyone else in Ipswich.

### ENGLISH VERSUS AMERICAN LANGUAGE

ALMOST before you meet the people you will hear them speaking "English." At first you may not understand what they are talking about and they may not understand what you say. The accent will be different from what you are used to, and many of the words will be strange, or apparently wrongly used. But you will get used to it. Remember that back in Washington stenographers from the South are having a hard time to understand dictation given by business executives from New England and the other way around.

In England the "upper crust" speak pretty much alike. You will hear the news broadcaster for the BBC (British Broadcasting Corporation). He is a good example, because he has been trained to talk with the "cultured" accent. He will drop the letter "r" (as people do in some sections of our own country) and will say "hyah" instead of "here." He will use the broad *a* pronouncing all the *a*'s in "Banana" like the *a* in "father." However funny you may think this is, you will be able to understand people who talk this way and they will be able to understand you. And you will soon get over thinking it is funny.

You will have more difficulty with some of the local dialects. It may comfort you to know that a farmer or villager from Cornwall very often can't understand a farmer or villager in Yorkshire or Lancashire. But you will learn—and they will learn—to understand you.

**Some Hints on British Words.** British slang is something you will have to pick up for yourself. But even apart

41

from slang, there are many words which have different meanings from the way we use them and many common objects have different names. For instance, instead of railroads, automobiles, and radios, the British will talk about railways, motorcars, and wireless sets. A railroad tie is a sleeper. A freight car is a goods wagon. A man who works on the roadbed is a navvy. A streetcar is a tram. Automobile lingo is just as different. A light truck is a lorry. The top of a car is the hood. What we call the hood (of the engine) is a bonnet. The fenders are wings. A wrench is a spanner. Gas is petrol—if there is any.

Your first furlough may find you in some small difficulties because of language difference. You will have to ask for sock suspenders to get garters and for braces instead of suspenders—if you need any. If you are standing in line to buy (book) a railroad ticket or a seat at the movies (cinema) you will be queuing (pronounced "cueing") up before the booking office. If you want a beer quickly, you had better ask for the nearest pub. You will get your drugs at a chemist's and your tobacco at a tobacconist, hardware at an ironmonger's. If you are asked to visit somebody's apartment, he or she will call it a flat.

A unit of money, not shown on the following page, which you will sometimes see advertised in the better stores is the guinea (pronounced "ginny" with the "g" hard as in "go"). It is worth 21 shillings, or one pound

## TABLE OF BRITISH CURRENCY

**Copper Coins**

| Symbol | Name | British value | American value (approximate) |
|---|---|---|---|
| ¼d. | farthing (rare) | ¼ penny | ½ cent. |
| ½d. | halfpenny ("hay-p'ny") | ½ penny | 1 cent. |
| 1d. | penny | 1 penny | 2 cents. |
| 3d. | threepence ("thruppence" or "thrup-'ny bit"; rare). | 3 pence | 5 cents. |

**Silver Coins**

| | | | |
|---|---|---|---|
| 3d. | threepence ("thruppence" or "thrup-'ny bit": not common in cities). | 3 pence | 5 cents. |
| 6d. | sixpence | 6 pence | 10 cents. |
| 1s. | shilling (or "bob") | 12 pence | 20 cents. |
| 2s. | florin (fairly rare) | 2 shillings | 40 cents. |
| 2s. 6d. | half crown (or "two and six"). | 2½ shillings | 50 cents. |
| 5s. | crown (rare) | 5 shillings | $1.00. |

**Paper Currency**

| | | | |
|---|---|---|---|
| 10s. | 10-shilling note | 10 shillings (or ½ pound). | $2.00. |
| 1 | pound note | 20 shillings | $4.00. |
| 5 | 5-pound note | 5 pounds | $20.00. |

plus one shilling. *There is no actual coin or bill of this value in use.* It is merely a quotation of price.

A coin not shown in the above table is the gold sovereign, with a value of one pound. You will read about it in English literature but you will probably never see one and need not bother about it.

WEIGHTS AND MEASURES: The measures of length and weight are almost the same as those used in America. The British have inches, feet, yards, pints, quarts, gallons, and so forth. You should remember, however, that the English (or "Imperial") gallon contains about one-fifth more liquid than the American gallon.

### SOME IMPORTANT DO'S AND DON'TS

BE FRIENDLY—but don't intrude anywhere it seems you are not wanted. You will find the British money system easier than you think. A little study beforehand on shipboard will make it still easier.

You are higher paid than the British "Tommy." Don't rub it in. Play fair with him. He can be a pal in need.

Don't show off or brag or bluster—"swank" as the British say. If somebody looks in your direction and says, "He's chucking his weight about," you can be pretty sure you're off base. That's the time to pull in your ears.

If you are invited to eat with a family don't eat too much. Otherwise you may eat up their weekly rations.

Don't make fun of British speech or accents. You sound just as funny to them but they will be too polite to show it.

Avoid comments on the British Government or politics.

Don't try to tell the British that America won the last war or make wisecracks about the war debts or about British defeats in this war.

NEVER criticize the King or Queen.

Don't criticize the food, beer, or cigarettes to the British. Remember they have been at war since 1939.

Use common sense on all occasions. By your conduct you have great power to bring about a better understanding between the two countries after the war is over.

You will soon find yourself among a kindly, quiet, hard-working people who have been living under a strain such as few people in the world have ever known. In your dealings with them, let this be your slogan:

*It is always impolite to criticize your hosts; it is militarily stupid to criticize your allies.*

radio—*wireless*
railway car—*railway carriage*
raincoat—*mackintosh, or mac, or waterproof*
roadster (automobile)—*two-seater*
roast (of meat)—*joint*
roller coaster—*switchback-railway*
rolling grasslands—*downs*
round trip—*return trip*
roomer—*lodger*
rooster—*cock, or cockerel*
rubbers—*galoshes*
rumble seat—*dickey*
run (in a stocking)—*ladder*
saloon—*public house, or pub*
scallion—*spring onion*
scrambled eggs—*buttered eggs*
second floor—*first floor*
sedan (automobile)—*saloon car*
sewerage (house)—*drains*
shoestring—*bootlace, or shoelace*
shot (athletics)—*weight*
shoulder (of road)—*verge*
rubberneck wagon—*char-a-banc*
silverware—*plate*
slacks—*bags*
sled—*sledge*
smoked herring—*kipper*
soda biscuit (or cracker)—*cream-cracker*
soft drinks—*minerals*
spark plug—*sparking-plug*
spigot (or faucet)—*tap*
squash—*vegetable marrow*

stairway—*staircase, or stairs*
string bean—*French-bean*
store—*shop*
subway—*underground*
sugar-bowl—*sugar-basin*
suspenders (men's)—*braces*
sweater—*pull-over*
syrup—*treacle*
taffy—*toffee*
taxi stand—*cab rank*
telegram—*wire*
tenderloin (of beef)—*under-cut, or fillet*
ten pins—*nine pins*
thumb-tack—*drawing pin*
ticket office—*booking office*
toilet—*lavatory, closet*
top (automobile)—*hood*
transom (of door)—*fanlight*
trolley—*tram*
truck—*lorry*
undershirt—*vest, or singlet*
union-suit—*combinations*
vaudeville—*variety*
vaudeville theatre—*music hall*
vest—*waistcoat*
vomit—*be sick*
washbowl—*washbasin*
washrag—*face cloth*
washstand—*wash-hand stand*
water heater—*geyser*
window shade—*blind*
"you're connected"—*"you're through"* (telephone)
windshield (automobile)—*windscreen*

## THE BRITISH THINK SO TOO

THE IDEA of getting together with the British in solid friendship isn't a one-sided proposition. They, as well as we, believe in the necessity of being Allies in the truest meaning of the word if we are to dish it out in full measure to Hitler.

As a matter of fact, the British started the idea of providing soldiers with guide books to help them understand their Allies. The first RAF cadets to come to the United States for training were given a little book called "Notes for Your Guidance" which told them how to get along with Americans.

Then, too, the British Army Bureau of Current Affairs issued a bulletin, "Meet the Americans," to men in the army. For your information on how the British think about this subject, a part of that Bulletin is reproduced on the next page.

his gang will do all they can to produce ill will between us. Our answer to that game is persistent, determined good will: the resolution to believe the best about people we don't yet know. It should be a matter of personal mental discipline to adopt this attitude.

**Respect:** Toward nations as toward individuals we must show respect for positive achievement. We may dislike a man's face or the cut of his clothes or his fashion in food—yet acknowledge him as a fine engineer or architect or musician. Respect for American achievement is one of the ways by which we shall discover the Americans. Look, for example, what they've done to refrigerators and combustion engines and acknowledge them as the world's inventive wizards.

**Patience:** If you want someone's friendship, don't snatch it; wait for it. Peoples as foreign to each other as the Americans and ourselves have a lot to learn before we reach understanding. The first necessity is to be informed about each other, to replace the film version and the story-book version by the real facts. We shall get the facts one way and one way only—by seeking them in a spirit of genuine interest.

Not even the most intensely nationalistic man or woman can resist that spirit. Ask a "foreigner" about his home town, what he likes to eat, where he works, what he does on Sunday, where he goes for his holidays, how his home is furnished, and so on—and you'll invariably achieve two things. You'll discover a lot about the land he comes from, and you'll make him feel you have a genuine interest in him. There and there only, without blah or baloney is the plain man's way to Anglo-American understanding.

The signal is "Get Acquainted." Never mind the vows and the flags and the keepsakes, for no alliance, whether national or matrimonial, ever survives on sentiment alone. We've got to understand and respect each other for two reasons. First, because we want to be real comrades in arms, not phoney ones of the Axis variety. Second, and even more important, we don't want a mere wartime friendship. We want the real thing—the alliance which survives the peace and becomes a permanent force in the shaping of the new world.

*From British Army Bureau of Current Affairs Bulletin, No. 22, July 18, 1942, "Meet the Americans."*

Some of those billeted here did not return to their families

Austin Chestnut from Ohio was billeted in Torcross at 'Windfalls House' He left the inscription below on the windowsill of that house.

Sadly he was later killed in France on 9th July 1944 but not before his tank had destroyed three enemy tanks.

# Exercise Tiger 28th April 1944

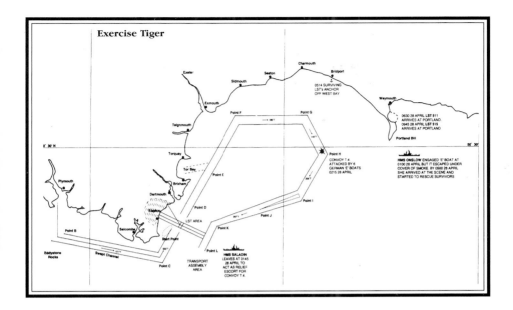

The convoy left Plymouth escorted by a destroyer, HMS Scimitar, and a corvette HMS Azalea. Unfortunately HMS Scimitar was rammed by one of the landing craft and was holed, so she had to return to Plymouth. HMS Azalea continued along as the convoy headed into Lyme Bay to give the soldiers the same time at sea as they would have to experience if they crossed the Channel to France.

The second problem was that all the convoy had received orders with a typing error, giving the wrong radio frequency to be used. So they had no communication with HMS Azalea or with HQ ashore both of whom were using the correct frequency. So when the flotilla of seven German E-boats was spotted on the radar of another destroyer off Portland Bill, there was no way to warn the LSTs in the convoy.

**At 2.00am on 28th April 1944**
The German E-boats torpedoed the convoy and sank LST 507 and LST 531. LST 289 was badly damaged, but managed to make it back to Dartmouth. The rest of the convoy continued with the planned assault of Slapton Beach. 749 dead is the official figure of men lost in the attack, but the actual number is believed to be much greater.

From a painting by S/M Ted Archer 1995.
Photograph by kind permission of Ian Davidson.

LST 289 Arrives back in Dartmouth to off load the dead and wounded. The damage from the E-boat's torpedo is so extensive it is amazing that the boat was able to reach port.

The full scale of Operation Tiger can be appreciated from the number of vessels within Start Bay, standing off Slapton Sands. Les Tabb from Slapton was on board one of the destroyers. You can only guess at his feelings seeing his home village being bombarded.

Naval ships shell selected targets on the beach and further inland. At the same time both fighter bombers and medium bombers attack other targets within the evacuated area.

To make the practice as real as possible the defenders were using live ammunition throughout the assault. Two hundred more lives were lost to friendly fire.

The infantry were the first to secure the beach head. Mine fields had been laid all along the base of the cliff and at intervals along the length of Slapton Sands.

Landings took place all along the beach. Torcross was protected by barbed wire in front of the village and a mine field where the main car park now stands.

Wave after wave of soldiers were landed on the beach before forcing their way inland.

Once the beach had been secured by the infantry, more equipment was landed.

As the practice battles moved further inland, the LSTs landed the heavier equipment.

Blackpool Sands became a landing stage for the fuel and supplies for the men and equipment used as the exercise continued.

More equipment arriving on Landcombe Cove between Strete and Blackpool Sands. Judging by the deep tracks on the beach the jeeps are obviously finding the shingle hard going.

The engineers also needed to refine their skills, so a pontoon bridge was built across the Ley from the site of the bombed Royal Sands Hotel to the shore on the South Ground Farm below Slapton village.

The popular story is that a mine field had been laid around the hotel and a stray dog wandered in and set off one of the mines and so destroyed the Royal Sands Hotel. However the American GI is standing in such a large crater on the beach that it is fairly obvious at least one bomb had been dropped and that a great many naval gun shells had probably helped to destroy the hotel.

# June 1944. Embarkation for D-Day in Dartmouth

The Britannia Royal Naval College was taken over as U.S. Navy Headquarters for the organisation of loading men and equipment from Dartmouth for the D-Day landings.

An American tank makes its way past Coronation Park which was used as a military depot.

Nissen huts and work sheds were built on Coronation Park, Dartmouth, to make sure all the army vehicles were in top condition ready for action.

The bridge over the entrance to the Boat Float was reinforced to take the military vehicles.

1st June 1944

Medium tanks and half tracks commenced loading onto a LST ready for the invasion of Normandy. Tanks are reversed onto the landing craft for a quick exit.

2nd June 1944

Personnel and equipment were loaded.  It was still unclear whether this was just another exercise so  everyone just had to wait for orders.

Soldiers waiting to embark on the landing craft on the Kingswear side of the River Dart.

## 3rd June 1944

Barrage balloons are tethered above the shipping in Dartmouth Harbour in case of a surprise attack by enemy aircraft as the armada is assembled.

*From a painting by Charles Baskerville, June 1944.*

The armada of over 480 craft starts to leave the harbour. There was a continuous stream of craft from midday until well into the evening. It was only when they got to sea that the men were told that this time it was 'the real thing'.

**Salcombe Harbour** - over sixty vessels left the estuary to join the convoys for the Normandy landings.

*Photograph courtesy of Capt. J.V.Waterhouse DSO. OBE. RN*
The slipway used for repairing the landing craft and the Nissen hut workshops on Millbay beach played an important role in preparing the fleet for crossing the Channel.

*Photograph by Capt. J.V.Waterhouse DSO. OBE. RN*
The boats were taken out of the water on a huge wheeled trestle guided by steel rail on a concrete ramp.

The build up and equipping of the Salcombe armada proceeded to the same time scale as in Dartmouth.

LSTs being loaded from the beach.

4th June 1944 (The operation was postponed for twenty four hours)

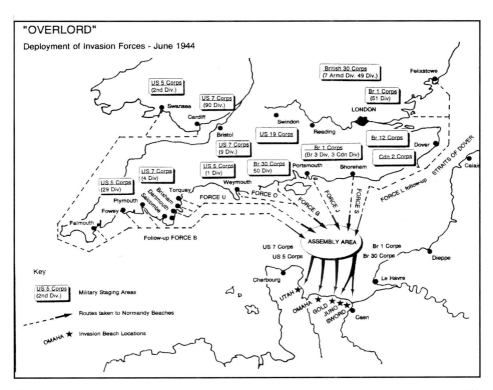

The weather was so bad that the invasion had to be cancelled for twenty four hours. All craft remained at sea in the assembly area off Weymouth. The landing craft were only designed for a maximum of twelve hours at sea so there was little or no shelter for the men on board. Most of the soldiers suffered from the cold and from sea sickness.

# 6th June 1944.  Operation Overlord
# D-Day
### The Normandy Beaches

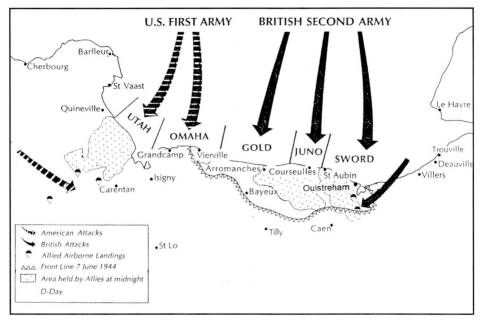

*Maps by kind permission of Ray Freeman 'We remember D-Day'*
The men that trained on Slapton Beach and in the evacuated area, were engaged in the attack on Utah and Omaha beaches. Casualties on Utah numbered two hundred, probably less than one fifth of those who lost their lives in 'Exercise Tiger', but casualties on Omaha were very high.

6th June 1944   (H-Hour had arrived for Operation Overlord)

Under cover of darkness the invasion fleet had approached the French coast. Between 2.00 a.m. and 3.00 a.m. the 'Seabee' contingent left the armada in small boats to secure strategic points. At 5.30am all craft in the armada opened fire on targets on the beach. One hour later at 6.30am the first landing craft arrived on the beach.

As well as heavy enemy fire the troops had to cope with obstacles and mine fields on the beaches.

As the battle moved inland more men and equipment arrived in ever greater numbers.

Soon the allies started taking prisoners of war, but there were many casualties on both sides.

# Damage in the area was extensive

After the soldiers and all their equipment had left, the seagulls and a plague of rats moved in to scavenge on all the scraps of food left behind by the American forces. The fenced area on the beach was one of the many mine fields.

The army bomb disposal squads were the first to return to the area. It was their job to clear the many unexploded shells, mines and other ordinance to make the area safe for the population to return. They were followed by the 'Civil Defence Mobile Reserve Workers',

whose job it was to tidy and repair the individual houses and to clear up items left behind by the billeted soldiers. However these men were perhaps too enthusiastic with their cleaning up and many private possessions left behind by the evacuees such as the brass fittings, door knobs and coat hooks vanished at this time.

Many local rat catchers were also allowed into the area to help clear the plague of rats that had thrived during the military occupation.

In the picture to the left, men from the C.D.M.R.W. can be seen removing the army camp beds from the Torcross Hotel. The building behind the lorry is the former Venture Guest House. Its thatched roof was destroyed by fire caused by tracer bullets used in exercises.

Stokenham Church and the Church House Inn were badly damaged during exercises.

The once elegant Manor House Hotel at Strete Gate had been used as one of the targets for the naval bombardment.

The damage was so severe that the hotel was never rebuilt. After being demolished it now forms the picnic area at the end of the beach.

The Manor House Hotel (above) was located at Strete Gate on the site adjacent to the car park.

The ruins can be seen at the bottom of the field. The damage caused by naval gun fire and by mortar bombs is typical of that suffered by many properties throughout the evacuated area. Inspectors from the ministry of housing recorded all the damage, but only paid compensation to the farmers and to businesses in the area. The private home owners received no compensation.

The gardeners' cottages and stables were also part of the Manor House Hotel but were situated on the other side of the road on the shore of the Upper Ley. These buildings were redeveloped to produce the present dwelling, the Manor, below.

The thatched cottages on the left included the blacksmith's forge, a private cottage, a boys' club and the village reading room. The thatch caught fire during Exercise Tiger and the premise was never rebuilt. The car park for the King's Arms pub now occupies the site.

**24th June 1954.** The dedication of the monument which was presented by the United States Army in gratitude to the people of the South Hams. Present were Lieutenant General John Lee, Commanding General of the Communications Zone, European Theatre of Operations and Sir John Daw, chairman of Devon County Council, who had the job of explaining to the local population why they had to leave their homes in 1943.

# THE EVACUATION — 1943-1944

**Reminiscences of some of the villagers from Blackawton, Chillington, East Allington, Sherford, Slapton, Stokenham, Strete and Torcross as told to Jean Parnell.**

Many books have been written about D-Day and the consequences but as far as I know, no book has been written solely of reminiscences and reactions of the villagers who were evacuated and those associated with the evacuation.

When I first had the idea of talking to those concerned with the view to making a few notes, I had no notion how successful this might prove. I have talked to residents of each village evacuated and I apologise for not having spoken to everyone! Most memories are bound to be similar, but each one has something individual about it.

I thank all these people for their interest, help, friendship and numerous cups of tea!

I thank Ken too for being so patient, not only for providing an excellent taxi service but for the hours I have spent putting pen to paper! The results are to be found in the following pages.　　　　　　　　　　　Jean Parnell

*I dedicate these pages to my great-nieces, Sarah and Lucy Ayling.*


With grateful thanks to Slapton Ley Field Centre for the work that has gone into the presentation of these reminiscences.


## Gladys Coe - nee Trant

During the early Autumn of 1943, Gladys was an eighteen year old living and working with her father and brother at Dittiscombe Farm, Slapton. They ran a mixed farm with six or seven working horses, cattle and chickens and grew corn, turnips and mangolds. They heard rumours of an evacuation from Jim Hewitt, a member of the Home Guard. At first they thought it was just a rumour but when notices giving details of meetings to be held were posted, they soon realised it was about to happen.

Gladys's father had no car but petrol was needed to run the machine which bruised and ground the corn. Petrol was obtained from East Allington and carried in a can strapped to the back of Gladys's bike. On one of these journeys she was astounded when she met a pack of mules with their Gurkha handlers. The Gurkhas were stationed in East Allington at Fallapit House. Whenever the vet was needed, a cycle ride to Torcross had to be made, carefully manoeuvring between rows of barbed wire and concrete anti-tank posts, mainly along the Line.

Before the Trants left Dittiscombe there was much activity in baling hay and straw from ricks made earlier in the year. Threshing corn and working hard in the granary filling two hundredweight sacks with corn meant working until 1.00 or 2 .00 a.m. in the morning for Gladys and her brother. Some of the cattle and horses were sold but most went with them to Rowden Farm, at Widecombe-in-the-Moor where Mr Trant remained. Land Army girls, some Irish men and Royal Navy personnel helped on the farm with packing and a lorry was at their disposal each day until dusk.

Pullets used to wander round the yard, gleaning any surplus grain and one evening when Gladys was going to shut them in, she realised they had disappeared! She and her father, in a friend's car, pursued the lorry transporting the sailors back to their billet at Stanborough House. En route they called at the Halwell Police House and with P.C. Rendle, caught up with the offenders at Moreleigh Bridge. There was the evidence in the lorry - feathers and fully plucked pullets ready to send to the sailors' families for Christmas. Apparently, Mr Trant dismissed the whole affair.

As there was still work to be done before vacating the farm, after most of the furniture had gone, the Trant family was allowed to stay over the Christmas period when the American GIs brought tins of food for their Christmas lunch. Gladys now lives in Totnes.

### Frances Goodman - nee Bond

In 1943, Frances was living with her family at Lower Poole Farm, East Allington. A year earlier, Frances arrived home late one night after helping at a canteen for British soldiers billeted in the village, just before four bombs were dropped nearby, killing three cows and injuring another four. A while later one of the farm workers discovered an unexploded bomb lodged at the foot of a hedge. The bomb was taken away for detonation by P.C. Rendle of Halwell, on the back seat of his Morris seven car!

The first the Bond family heard of the evacuation was from Frank White, a Special Constable living at Hansel. When Mr Bond heard it, his first reaction was 'They'll never do it', but before long they realised it actually was to be.

Lower Poole was a mixed farm and much of the stock was sold at one of two special livestock sales at Kingsbridge. On leaving day, the last meal was a fry-up of food left over and after cooking it they discovered although they had cups, cutlery and the frying pan, they had no plates, so they all ate from the communal frying pan!

Frances and her family spent the next few months at a friend's farmhouse in Harbertonford. They lived in the servants' entrance hall , had two bedrooms and the butler's pantry. As most of their furniture was in store, they bought an oil stove on which to cook. Mr Bond took his tractor and helped on the farm. They managed to take one cow for her milk and a sow named Jezebel, as she was about to produce piglets. A farmer at Hatchlands, near Rattery, took the working horses.

As a thirteen year old, Colin, one of the sons, remembers crying over the loss of his favourite cow, Negus, which had to be sold. His brother Tony remembers the public meeting held in East Allington Church, although he was only ten years old. Apparently, they had about a dozen cows, forty ewes and twenty ewe lambs, all of which were sold, except the cow which they took with them. The cows made about £40 each and the ewes £7 or £8 each.

When the Bonds returned to Lower Poole in September 1944, the boys were thrilled to find the yard full of rabbits - but their father wasn't so thrilled! Auctioneers came to value the property to assess compensation and they found little damage had been done structurally. Door panels had been removed and possibly used as firewood. All the rooms were very dirty and had to be scrubbed with a stiff broom and hot water, and for this, one shilling (5p) per room was allowed!

The sons said that East Allington was like a ghost town in 1944 - no-one in the fields, church bells silent and every house empty. Fields and gardens were overgrown and crops like turnips had gone to seed. On the day before the villagers returned, one hundredweight. of coal was delivered to each house to help the fires get rid of the dampness.

Later, the boys farmed with their father on the land which has been in the Bond Family for over a hundred years, and continue to do so. Frances still lives there too.

### Colin Bond

Another Colin Bond was a very young boy living with his parents at Higher Collaton Farm, Blackawton, between the Forces Tavern and Halwell Barn. This farm was in the unique position of being part in, part out of the requisitioned area and in fact one field was used for their chickens and another by the U.S. troops to pitch the field-kitchen tents. About half the farm's acreage was lost.

Colin says he doesn't remember much about the soldiers being there, but he does remember a rick, made of bundles of straw, being pulled apart by some of them to use as bedding. One night some of the troops came into the farmhouse and pumped the well dry! He says he does remember the soldiers giving the children sweets.

Several years ago, a phosphorous bomb, which had survived since the evacuation resting on a hedge, rolled into the road and the Bomb Disposal Unit had to be called to deal with it.

### Brian Tucker

When Brian Tucker's family living at Combe Farm, Blackawton, heard rumours and then facts about the evacuation, he said they were all in a complete state of shock. Nevertheless they set about baling hay and preparing cattle for one of the special auctions for surplus stock held in Totnes.

Brian and his brother Gordon were registered contractors so they were allowed a certain amount of T.V.O. (tractor vapour oil) to continue carrying out their agricultural work. During the evacuation they lived in part of Bramble Tor Farmhouse, Dittisham with the Webber family. They took with them three working horses and cattle, mangolds, hay and straw. The hay and straw were stored in a hayloft.

As the Tuckers were tenant farmers they were advised to give up the tenancy, but they refused as this might have meant not being able to return to the same farm. Some damage was done to the farmhouse and thousands of rounds of unused bullets were found in ricks round about. Compensation for 'dilapidation' was paid by the Admiralty after their return.

### The late Herbert Luscombe

In the days before the Second World War most villages had a blacksmith. At Stokenham in 1943 the blacksmith was Herbert Arthur Luscombe and he said his first reaction when hearing of the evacuation was that it had to happen. He took his tools and smithy equipment to Beeson where he shared the blacksmith's shop. There was less work for him as the farms nearby with working horses were evacuated too.

Herbert was a member of the Home Guard and each night they went to watch the coast. He remembers the American troops being friendly with the local people and generous in giving sweets to the young children and cigarettes to the men. Someone left a Baby Austin car at Widewell near Torcross and the Americans, having access to petrol, used to drive around in it! Apparently, there was much looting between the time of the Americans' departure and the residents' return. Scrap iron which had been left in the smithy was stolen. No compensation was paid to blacksmiths for loss of earnings during the evacuation. Boxes of dynamite and ammunition were left in barns and fields round about.

Herbert returned to Stokenham and to his smithy late in 1944, a living in a cottage next door to his blacksmith's shop. He passed away in the late 1990s.

## A Land Army Girl

One lady living in the district was in the Land Army during 1943 earning twenty two shillings and six pence per week, out of which had to come money for lodgings. She said the G.I.s mixed well with the locals and there were always parties being held to which the local girls were invited. She actually went inside the requisitioned area to collect fruit which was rotting on the bushes and trees, and she said there was a feeling of eerie quietness everywhere. On the farm where she was working until the evacuation, the cows upon their return, each went into their own stall in the milking-parlour at milking time!

## May and Bill Elliott

May and Bill Elliott's reactions to being told of the evacuation were the same as many other residents - 'They'll never do it'.

Bill worked at Stokeley Farm Stokenham. One day while he and his father-in-law, Willoughby Yalland, were cutting corn with a horse and binder, a German fighter aircraft machine gunned the field and luckily they were near enough to a hedge to take cover. Nevertheless the bullets chipped pieces of wood from the handles of the prongs they had been using.

Bill too was a member of the Home Guard and while patrolling the coast in the evenings their base was the Crowing Cock Restaurant Torcross (opposite the main car park). Gates at Torcross and Strete Gate were closed each night and only those people carrying special permits were allowed through. Evidently, Home Guard members often spent their evenings in a tin hut on the Ley side of the Line, with British soldiers. One night a soldier threw a live cartridge into the coke brazier which livened things up a bit!

The Elliotts found a job at Blakemore Farm near Totnes with a house and garden, so they were able to take chickens with them and their pet cat. Their belongings were transported by tractor and trailer. During their time at Blakemore, milk from the farm was collected by a G.W.R. lorry and this lorry also collected milk from farms adjacent to the restricted area in the South Hams.

One driver offered to take May and Bill back to Stokenham, where they found the roads covered with glass, garden walls holed, the church and the Church House Inn in need of re-roofing. They said that there was a quiet, weird feeling and they heard no birds singing.

When they finally returned there was much tidying up to do and everyone set about this task willingly. Most families did return to Stokenham where the Elliotts lived until 1999, when they moved to Malborough.

## The Hannaford Family

The Hannaford family has had a butchery business in Torcross for over a hundred years. Reg, one of the brothers still at the butcher's shop, was only fourteen when news of the evacuation was made known and he remembers at one of the meetings, an American General promised that no wanton damage would be done to churches, while places of historical interest would be clearly marked.

Reg and his family moved to a farm at Chivelstone for the duration of the evacuation and as half the family's butcher's round was inside the restricted area, business was poor. They were able to rent a lock-up shop in Prawle, but the biggest snag was there was no electricity. They took laying hens with them, and as meat was rationed, they had no need for very large storage rooms.

When they left Torcross their means of transport to Chivelstone was a meat lorry driven by Bill Hurley of Stoke Fleming. After the household effects were loaded, the chicken sheds came next and lastly, bags of coke on the tailboard with Reg sitting on top! Reg's father had to leave the family car, a Rover, behind, and when they returned to Torcross it was discovered in the Ley!

The large yard at the rear of the butcher's shop was used by the troops as a tank park. Buildings had been demolished and a large meat-chopping block was found, half burnt, under a slab. Mr Hannaford had taken off brass door knobs and knockers and hidden them in a barn, but those had disappeared when they returned - most likely, after the exercises had finished.

Reg remembers much broken glass laying about, not only the effects of shelling, but because rats became particularly partial to the putty which had been used to replace the broken panes before householders returned. Most residents of Torcross did come back, but there are not many left now.

## Joy Heath - nee Deller

At the beginning of the war, Joy Deller was living in Paignton with her parents doing secretarial work. In 1941 she wondered whether to work in a munition's factory or join the Land Army. Having decided on the latter, she went to Seale Hayne Agricultural College the following year, where she did the one month's obligatory training, rising each morning at 5.30 a.m. to do the milking.

Joy's first farm was Keynedon Barton, Frogmore, a farm run by the Heath family. She said she remembers feeling very lucky as she lived with and was treated as one of the family. There was a tractor, working horses, cows, fat bullocks and sheep. The animals were her special interest. Potatoes, cauliflowers, swedes and mangolds were grown and she says the season for harvesting was particularly wet in 1943.

After news of the evacuation broke, the Heath family moved to a holiday home in Thurlestone. Cows went to Aveton Gifford, sheep went to Prawle and with the help of sailors and a gang of Land Army girls, hay and straw were taken from the ricks, baled and put into storage in barns at Charleton. One of the farmer's sons, William (later to become Joy's husband), transported fodder to the farms. Chickens were taken to Thurlestone, except one old hen which remained at Frogmore and was still there, scratching about in the yard when the family returned in August 1944.

On a wall in a panelled room in Keynedon Barton were two sets of antlers with skeletal heads. Mrs Heath took them down and placed them in a cupboard , which was securely locked. One day while Joy and William were in Kingsbridge, two tank transporters were passing through, and there on the front of each was a set of antlers, painted red and wreathed with American 'pillar' roses.

On their return, the pet cat Tiddles made a return journey to Thurlestone where he had been fussed over by a couple of old ladies! The first task was to make hay even though it was late summer. Fields had to be cleared of mangolds and turnips which had gone to seed. There was little structural damage as the farm was a fair distance from the coastal bombardment but there were many 'foxholes' in the fields which had to be filled in.

Joy said help from the Admiralty was appreciated and farmers were paid compensation for 'dilapidation'. She remembers gifts on their return - a doormat, patchwork quilts and even a bucket and mop - an absolute necessity. Joy and William Heath now live in Chillington.

## The Late Tom Brooking and Winnie Brooking

Tom and Winnie Brooking of Chillington had married just about a year before the evacuation. Unfortunately, Tom passed away in 1988, but Winnie remembers their reactions. At first they felt upset at having to leave, but realised they were luckier than many who had been bombed out of their homes losing everything - at least they could take their possessions with them.

Winnie says the parish church at Stokenham was packed to capacity with those under notice to leave, and explanations were given by the Lord Lieutenant of Devon, Earl Fortescue and General Gruenther, Supreme Commander Allied Forces Europe based in Paris with S.H.A.E.F. (Supreme Headquarters Allied Expeditionary Force). They told the residents that American troops were to engage in immense military exercises. The responses ranged from broken-hearted among the elderly, to excited anticipation among the children. The over-riding questions were - 'Where will we go' and 'How will we get there?'

An information and organisation centre was set up in Stokenham Parish Hall. When people were ready to leave they locked all the doors and handed in the keys, tied and labelled.

Tom had a building business which had to close, but he did carry on with building at Prawle where he and Winnie spent the evacuation at Woodcombe Farm. The couple lived in a wooden bungalow owned by Nurse Rendle and at night they frequently heard German planes passing over en route to bomb Plymouth. They were never short of food, Winnie remembers, and realised that country people had greater advantages over town folk in this respect. Their means of transport was a bicycle but there was an infrequent bus service to Kingsbridge. Many coloured U.S. servicemen were stationed in and around Prawle and they were always most polite and friendly towards the Devonians.

After about nine months, Tom and Winnie returned to Chillington to find their home dirty but undamaged. In Stokenham the church and the Church House Inn were badly affected by shelling. Tom's employees repaired both and he was asked by the land agents Luscombe Maye to value and assess properties for compensation. Starting up again in the village was no problem and Winnie still lives there.

## The Late Eva and Bert Yalland

Eva and Bert Yalland were living in Strete in 1942 with their daughters Jean and Margaret. In March of that year a German Focke-Wulf fighter aircraft came down in Waypark Lane very near their home. The plane was one of a group which flew over the sea too low on a foggy evening then had to rise when the cliffs loomed ahead. The Bofors gun sited at the cliff top fired and, it is thought, injured the pilot. The aircraft flew over the village to crash in flames and the pilot was killed.

The first the Yallands heard of the evacuation was when public notices were placed in the village. Margaret, who was only five, wondered why everyone had to be 'vaccinated'. The evacuees who had been in the village had returned home by November 1943 as it was considered safe for them to return to Bristol.

It was not easy finding work with a house but eventually Eva's cousin who lived at Tigley, near Dartington heard of a job on a nearby farm with a cottage. This was at a hamlet called Brooking and was a thatched place with a stream running past. It was fairly comfortable but at night rats could be heard running in the roof. Apart from this the dwelling was warm and had a reasonably sized garden which produced a selection of vegetables.

Hundreds of U.S. troops were stationed in the fields all around and they were generous and friendly. Often tins of meat and fruit and wrapped parcels of bacon were discovered in a cardboard box on the doorstep in the early morning. Opposite was a farm where the Americans used to fill large baths each day with their waste food as pig swill. Frequently, tins of food and even uncooked chickens, carefully wrapped, were found in a special bath strategically placed under cover and out of sight!

About a week before D-Day, buses were taken off and there was a feeling of expectancy among the local people and troops. There was much activity in the fields - tents were dismantled, lorries, tanks and amphibious vehicles were prepared for moving out. Relatives evacuated and living in Stoke Fleming said that Dartmouth harbour and in fact the whole of Start Bay was full of craft of every description. Late on the 4th of June and for the next twenty four hours there was a steady flow of vehicles towards either Torbay or Dartmouth. The fields were once more deserted and woods bearing the tracks of many tanks, which had been well camouflaged, were empty again.

The family returned to Strete in January 1945, glad to be home even though there was much cleaning to do and clearing of gardens which had literally gone to seed. They were thankful too to have been welcomed in their temporary home.

Bert died in 1948 and until her death in 1998, Eva continued to live in Strete where Jean still lives.

## The Late Mr and Mrs Tom Luscombe

Mr and Mrs Tom Luscombe, daughter Freda and son Gordon lived at Sloutts Farm, Slapton. Another son, Ted was serving in the Royal Navy in 1943.

The Luscombes first heard about the evacuation from Mr and Mrs Lambert who kept the shop in the Roundhouse. American officers had hinted at this but everyone thought it was only a rumour and impossible.

When the news was made known, Mr Luscombe took advice and immediately tried to find somewhere to put the animals. He managed to find accommodation in Littlehempston at a farm where the farmer was willing to let two bedrooms, a sitting room and a shared kitchen. Feeding stuff - mangolds mainly - was taken to Muckwell Farm, Hallsands for winter feed for bullocks. Some cattle were sold in Kingsbridge.

## Freda and Tony Widger

Freda went to Muckwell Farm, the home of her fiancé, Tony Widger, and was able to help out there. It was a mixed farm milk round, they were the last to leave Slapton and the first to return.

From Muckwell it was possible to see ships in Start Bay firing and to hear shells going overhead. Freda says each time she wondered whose home was being hit. She and Tony married at the end of May, 1944, in Paignton Parish Church and continued living at Hallsands. One day Tony and a friend hedge-hopped back to Slapton to 'see what was happening' and visited Poole Farm where he and Freda were to settle after the evacuation. When he returned he said he didn't think it could be made habitable - buildings were badly damaged, there were holes in the roof and shell holes in the lawn to say nothing of shell holes in the fields - one of which had two hundred. Payment for filling these in was later made. While in Slapton, Tony picked raspberries to take home from a field at Brandis Park.

In November 1944, the family returned to Sloutts Farm. Freda and Tony lived there too as there was much work to be done at Poole before anyone could move in. They had been back three weeks before anyone else. There was no electricity supply, so they had to borrow oil lamps and water had to be fetched from across the road. Their bread came from Loddiswell as the Powlesland family had not yet returned to the bakery in Slapton.

As many unexploded shells were still in the fields and, it was thought, mines too, Mr Luscombe put sixty bullocks roaming the farm as mine detectors. Shells and thousands of bullets were found in all the fields. Hedges had been taken down and in some places replaced with fences and a track ran from the farm to the beach.

One day before the actual move back to Sloutts, Freda and a friend were cleaning the farmhouse and went to the rainwater butt, their only source of water at that time, and were amazed to see, coming from their garden, workmen with six baskets of apples from Sloutts garden! Freda said she wasn't sure who was most surprised. After this the workmen, who were supposed to be repairing damaged properties didn't return.

After about three months, Poole Farm was ready, and Tony and Freda built up stock and moved in. Tony had already planted cabbage plants, but these had been devoured by the hundreds of rabbits which seemed to be everywhere. Turnips in the field had gone to seed and although the fields were cleared, turnips were still coming up five years afterwards.

Tony and Freda retired some years ago and now live in a bungalow 'next door' to Poole Farm. In May 2004, they celebrate their Diamond Wedding.

## Miss Barbara Stroud

*This extract was written by Miss Barbara Stroud.*

In 1942, Assistant Section Officer Barbara Stroud took over as Officer in Charge of an R.A.F./W.A.A.F unit in Strete and was billeted for a year with Major and Mrs Chandler at Homelands - a charming house with a beautiful garden. The Chandlers' daughter Joyce also lived there. The family had a monkey of uncertain temperament - Sally was her name and although gentle with children, not with adults. Each Monday, Mrs Chandler made rabbit curry for the main meal - rather hot as she and her husband lived in India for many years. The dessert was blackberry and apple pie.

On 26th March 1994, after a break of fifty two years Miss Stroud came through Strete en route to Poole where she now lives, returning from a couple of days in Plymouth. She called at Homelands for old times' sake but found no-one in. It was suggested she should call on Mrs Parnell and these notes are the result.

Miss Stroud recalled that in March 1942 she went into the dining-room at Homelands and saw an aeroplane coming straight towards the house. It gained height fortunately and was a German tip-and-run fighter which was brought down by a Bren gun. Her unit had a Bren gun but the Army claimed the victory.

Miss Stroud has very happy memories of her wartime stay in Strete.

## Gordon Luscombe

Gordon was seventeen in 1943 working on his father's farm Sloutts. He remembers residents taking the attitude that there was a war on, they had to leave and that was that. Spirits were pretty low but people were prepared to make the best of it.

As there was insufficient work on the farm where his parents were living at Littlehempston, Gordon tried to join the Royal Navy, like his brother, but he was directed into working for a farm contractor. Much of the time he drove a lorry carrying fleeces to a woollen mill in Cornwall. The fleeces had to be collected from farms in Brixham and Kingswear and often these were not ready and there was no help in loading either - consequently, by the time the day's delivery was complete it was dark before Gordon reached home. Driving through Plymouth with scarcely any headlights and with no signposts anywhere was not the most enviable task. On some occasions Gordon had to go to the mill foreman's home to get him to open the warehouse before unloading his lorry.

One day in late summer 1944, Gordon sneaked back into Slapton from Blackawton, parts of which had been made safe and people had returned. Slapton was like a ghost town and the only person he met was P.C.Betts, the village policeman who was there to stop looters coming in. When he asked Gordon what he was doing, Gordon replied "The same as you, picking apples, pears and grapes that are going to waste". In the basket in the front of the cycle Gordon could see freshly picked grapes! While in Slapton Gordon had a look at their farmhouse but luckily it had not been damaged, although it was very dirty.

The Luscombe family was the first to return and Gordon recalls the Augean task of clearing and cleaning the lavatory - after a year with no mains water for flushing. After electricity and water supplies were fixed, the residents began to return and the milk round resumed

Much ammunition was left round about the farm and fields - live shells, hand grenades, mortar bombs. These were picked up and were collected each week by members of the Bomb Disposal Squad. Sometimes, workers on the farm would pull out the pin of hand grenade and throw it against the hedge - many would blow up, but not all. Once, while ploughing, Gordon disturbed a mortar bomb and just saw the fins before the tractor passed over it and it exploded! In the barns, U.S. Ration Packs in their boxes were found.

Gordon said a lot of people did not return and although it is still a good place to live he feels the spirit never quite recovered. In 1944 the whole nation seemed wholly united. Gordon still lives in Slapton, with his wife Marlene and has now retired from farming.

## The Late Allen Efford

When the local policemen and Special Constables were called to a meeting at Strete Police Station in the late summer of 1943, they were told of the plans for the evacuation, by Inspector Moore.

Allen Efford was one of the 'specials' who patrolled the village and surrounding area every night. In 1942, when a Focke- Wulf crashed, he and Police Constable Lake were enlisted to watch over the remains of the dead pilot until the body was recovered by the R.A.F. the next day.

One moonlit night, he and P.C.Winsor from Slapton were chatting with British soldiers (the Buffs) in a field near Turnpike Cottages (now Harbour Lights) in Strete when they noticed the periscope and underwater silhouette of a German submarine. Apparently the soldiers were keen to fire their gun but were stopped by P.C. Winsor who realised this would have alerted the Germans to their presence. There was a mystery about a man who lived in a flat at Blindwells, Strete. At night a light was visible coming from a chimney and after some time, the police went to investigate. The reception was unsociable and the man disappeared a couple of days later! He was later arrested in Paignton but no information was forthcoming.

Allen, his wife and baby daughter Jill found a cottage on the outskirts of Paignton where Allen worked on a farm. He returned to Strete one day before D-Day on his push bike and he noticed the brass front door bell had been stolen! As many others have said, the village was eerily quiet.

When the Efford family returned, the cottage was dirty but little damage had been done. Allen went to work for Mr and Mrs Knight at Higher Fuge Farm. There were shell holes to fill in but no arms nor ammunition were found. One day while ploughing, Allen ploughed up a mortar bomb which the Bomb Disposal Unit took away.

Gradually, village life got back to normal. The two shops, bakeries, butchers and cobblers all re-opened. Allen's wife, Kathleen, died in 1992 and Allen died in 2000. Jill, their daughter, now lives in Glastonbury.

## Mary Tucker - nee Lister

Mary Lister was an eighteen year old in 1943 living with her parents at Bunkers Farm, East Allington. For several years she had helped out on the farm delivering milk before catching the bus to school in Kingsbridge. Her parents heard of the evacuation and were convinced it was only a rumour until the official meeting in the village on November 13th.

Before actually leaving there was much to do - pulling mangolds to store them, baling straw and hay - jobs which were done with help from Land Army girls. The Listers found a farmer in Cornworthy who was prepared to let them have half the farmhouse accommodation and pasture for their cows. Mary remembers they all rode horses from East Allington to their new, temporary home.

Mary and Bill Lister returned to East Allington eight months later and they were the first farmers to return. Soon the cows too had settled and Mary resumed the milk round in the village shortly afterwards. The pub, the Fortesque Arms, reopened and stories of the last few months were exchanged. The only villager who had been officially allowed to walk round the village during the evacuation was Nathanial Williams. He was appointed Range Warden and his job was to see there was no-one in the village when the guns began firing. It was quite a while before he paid for his own drinks, people were only too keen to hear his anecdotes.

Mary met Gordon Tucker after the evacuation when he was working with his brother Brian as an agricultural contractor. There was much work for the brothers, as many fields had to be prepared for re-tilling after being unattended for so many months. Holes had to be filled and the ammunition left in fields to be disposed of.

Mary and Gordon married in 1947. Gordon died in 2002 and Mary now lives in Totnes.

## The Bowles Family

The Bowles family has been in Slapton for many years and when Margaret (now deceased), one of the seven children, heard in the village shop about the evacuation, her mother told her not to talk such rubbish - it just couldn't be done!

Mr and Mrs Bert Bowles took some time to find work with accommodation and eventually left their cottage in Brook Street and moved into part of the farmhouse at Milton Farm, Dartmouth. Mr and Mrs White the owners, let them have one downstairs room and two bedrooms. Mr Bowles worked on the farm.

Eddie and Mike, two of the youngest sons went to school in Dartmouth and walked through Waterpool, down into the town from Deadman's Cross. Eddie recalls watching planes exercising over Start Bay and the town being full of American soldiers while the harbour was full of ships of every description. He also remembers one afternoon coming home from school, soldiers sitting or lying in the hedge, complete with their arms and ammunition stretching from beyond Deadman's Cross down into the town.

Betty, one of the daughters, had worked in Powleslands Bakery, in Slapton which was next door to the Queen's Arms. As the Powleslands moved to Loddiswell during the evacuation, Betty went with her parents to Dartmouth. She had to go to the Labour Exchange to find work and decided on a job in an aircraft factory at Corsham and later at Bishops Cleeve. This helped a little with the accommodation at Milton Farm.

At the top of Milton Lane was an American camp and the Americans were generous towards the local people. There were several barrage balloons in the field and Eddie remembers one breaking away - the rope by which it was attached was made of strong rubber strands and when unravelled the rubber made marvellous catapults! This field was where the heliport now is situated.

Parts for assembling tanks were brought in large wooden crates and the soldiers passed the wood over the hedge, with Eddie 'on guard'. His uncle was an undertaker and builder so the wood was sold to him by an entrepreneurial nephew. Many lorries in Dartmouth had newly boarded floors as well.

Mike, the youngest of the family wasn't keen to live in Dartmouth at all and on the first night in their new, temporary home he cried wanting to go home and he didn't want the cold chicken either. He probably had a change of heart when the Americans gave him sweets and chocolate later on.

In early Autumn 1944, the Bowles family returned to Slapton - Eddie said it looked Like a deserted ghost town with doors creaking and rats all around. There were also plenty of rabbits which the children caught and sold around the village. One of his regrets was the disappearance of a small but treasured traction engine which used to drive a Meccano set. This had been left under the stairs but was obviously stolen.

Mike, with his wife Pat still lives in Slapton. Eddie with his wife Cathy moved from Slapton to Chillington in 2003. Arthur died in 1998, but his widow Peggy, still lives in Slapton. Betty married Les Tabb who was brought up in Slapton and spent the war years as a cook in the Royal Navy. Les died in 1999.

## The Late Godfrey Wills

Godfrey Wills of Asherne Cottages, Strete said his initial reaction on hearing of the evacuation was that there was a war on, people expected anything to happen and they took things as they came.

The Wills family has had a building business in Strete for nearly two hundred years. Godfrey, Emmie his wife, their daughters Pauline and Pam were the last people to leave the village. Their furniture was placed in a store in Torquay so they were reduced to a soap-box for a table, smaller boxes for seats, mattresses on the floor and a Primus stove for cooking. Shortly before leaving, Pauline recalls, her parents and a friend finished what was left of a twenty year old bottle of home-made parsley wine.

The family moved to Higher Farm, Beeson for the evacuation and Godfrey, with the help of Harry Skinner one of his workmen from Strete, was able to do some repairs and other building work. As Godfrey had belonged to the Royal Observer Corps at Blackhouse, Stoke Fleming, he transferred to the post at Start Point, just outside the requisitioned area. He remembers just a few days before D-Day dozens of LST's (landing craft), bunched together in Start Bay waiting for the weather to ease and for the sea to calm down. He says he felt very sorry for the troops in those conditions.

The officer in charge at Start Point was a Captain Primrose who was the owner of a very powerful telescope. With this it was possible to see troop movements as far away as Strete Gate, Godfrey thinks at one stage there were several injured troops as after one incident of shell and small arms fire, many ambulances were rushing from the shore along the Line - possibly to hospital.

In Widecombe Woods, behind Torcross, waterproofing of tanks took place. The tank parts came in wooden containers packed in something similar to fibreglass, were assembled and then waterproofed. In Widecombe House and Hallsands Hotel, American servicemen lived, with the officers and batmen at Hallsands. All the servicemen treated the local people well and often gave 'jeepsful' of ham to the fishermen. As the Royal Observer Corps volunteers were given strong Zeiss binoculars they could see the three rocket ships pitching their rockets landwards regularly.

The Beesands and Hallsands fishermen were allowed to fish as long as they did not stray east of Start Point. The 'Cricket Inn' at Beesands kept open but they were rationed to twenty eight gallons of beer per day. Apparently the landlord said that as beer was our national drink it should be kept for the locals. The Americans, fortunately, liked cider and some drank as many as a dozen pints each night.

Godfrey had a permit to go through the evacuated area after the Americans had gone. In September 1944 he picked apples from an orchard at Landcombe, Strete, as they were wasting.

When the Wills family returned to Strete soon after, they found their cottage undamaged except for broken panes of glass. Godfrey resumed work and before long their business was running as usual and there was no shortage of work.

Pam still lives at Asherne Cottages but Godfrey died in 1995. Pauline, who with her late husband Gordon Harris ran the Green Dragon Inn at Stoke Fleming, died in 2003.

## The Late Pauline Harris - nee Wills

Pauline Harris remembers taking Myrtle and Richard Cuming From Beeson, in a pony and trap to deliver milk around the village and to the U.S. camp. The children were always thrilled as the soldiers gave them chocolate and sweets - unobtainable at the time to British children.

Before being evacuated, Pauline with the help of May Jeffery, the infant teacher at Strete School at that time, helped run the Club in the village. It had formerly been for boys only but was opened to girls just after the war began. The Club also welcomed R.A.F. personnel who were billeted in the village and who paid one shilling and three pence (6p) per week to join. Pauline particularly remembers one who was older than most of them and he came so regularly they called him 'Old Faithful'.

The Club was part of the thatched properties which were destroyed during the evacuation - now the Kings Arms' car park. The room was quite small and had a beautifully carved fireplace - made by a Miss Keeling who came to the area for summer holidays. Pauline's mother, Emmie, used to light the fire in the middle of the afternoon, ready for the evening. Tea and biscuits used to be served and darts, table tennis and cards were played between the Royal Air Force and the British Army. Pauline and May also collected a few books to start a library - the loan charge was two pence per book. Once a month, Mrs Pearson who lived at Strete Lodge gave prizes for a whist drive held in the W.I. Reading Room next door to the Club.

One evening one of the airmen got quite a shock as he was passing the churchyard on the way back to his billet at the Crest. He and his mates were in the habit of saying 'Goodnight, Rosie' as they passed a headstone with the name of Rosie on it and on this particular night, a voice answered 'Good-night' - a courting couple had been standing in the school doorway (now the small doorway on the road in the Laughing Monk Restaurant).

Pauline said she and her family were very glad to be back in Strete again. She passed away in 2003.

## The Hyne Family

The Hyne family moved into Southwood Farm in 1940, William George was the farmer and he and his wife lived in the farm as did one of the sons Tom and his wife Emily. Another son also worked there - Bill, and he and his wife Mary and their children Peggy (now Edgecombe, died 2003), Jack and Pat (now Rowe), lived at Turnpike Cottages , Strete.

Tom remembered his father going to the meeting at Blackawton where he heard of the evacuation and on returning, set about finding farmers who might take some of the cows and working horses. Some of the hay and roots were taken to Pleasant Valley Farm, near Blackpool as were some of the cattle. Tom and his wife were to live in part of the farmhouse at Pleasant Valley with Mr and Mrs Lawson and Mr Phillips at Stoke Fleming took two of the cows. Mrs Hyne senior was taken ill during the evacuation and was in hospital at the Stoke Fleming Rectory, where she later died. Dartmouth Hospital was evacuated to Stoke Fleming for part of the war.

While they were evacuated Tom recalls a shell coming near to Venn, outside the evacuated area - it had obviously gone astray. Tom was in the Home Guard and he sometimes had to go through Stoke Fleming to the top of Frogmore Hill, skirting the requisitioned area.

Tom and family returned to Southwood in October 1944 and they found the house fairly clean and already repaired - the roads were not in such good order as they were full of potholes and uneven surfaces - the removal vans carrying their furniture could travel only on the main road, then the furniture had to be carried across the fields!

Emily died some years ago and Tom remained at Southwood until 1974. Tom and his sister Muriel spent their last years at Hinetown Residential Home where they both died during the 1990s.

## The Late Keeper Dean

I recently received a letter from Ron Atkinson of North Vancouver, British Columbia, whose uncle Walter Dean was the official rat-catcher in the requisitioned area after the Americans had left. This is part of his letter:-

"When I first visited Slapton I was sixteen and this was in 1942. Uncle Walter was the gamekeeper on the estate near Slapton. He lived in France Cottage in France Woods and moved later to Start Ridge Cottage where he lived at the time of the evacuation.

Everyone knew him as Keeper Dean and when the soldiers had left the evacuated area he was called upon to rid the area of rats. He was the first person to move back while his wife and family stayed in Paignton.

I also visited him in the summer of 1943 - Slapton Beach was then out of bounds because of mines and the Americans practising. I recall the Hotel (Royal Sands Hotel) that was located on the beach near the Monument erected in 1954. I remember too the big gun on the ridge above Torcross - the concrete emplacement remains.

In February 1994, we were on vacation in Arizona and met an American who was the driver of a Sherman tank. This man was in Plymouth a week before D-Day. We sent him a photograph of the tank at Torcross and a copy of 'The Forgotten Dead' by Ken Small."

I knew Walter Dean and his wife quite well and the couple spent their last years in a bungalow at Greenbanks Close, Slapton.

## Ken Parnell

Ken says this is not really about the evacuation but indirectly it is. When they left Strete in December 1943 his parents went to Cranacombe Cottages, on the Hazelwood Estate at Loddiswell, where his father worked on a farm. Ken had by this time joined the Royal Navy and been on the Isle of Man for boys' training. The time came for leave and Ken with Tony Bennett who now lives in Slapton and 'Dickie' Doyle from Kingsbridge arrived at Totnes Station one dark, rainy night to discover the last train to link up with the train for Kingsbridge had already left. This was Saturday night and the next train was not until Monday morning.

They were lucky enough to find a taxi and the driver said he would take them to Kingsbridge then take Ken on to Loddiswell.

They reached Kingsbridge and the taxi driver took Ken on to Loddiswell, or so Ken thought. As it was getting late, he decided to ask at the pub which was nearby, how to get to Cranacombe. The landlord had already gone to bed but assured Ken he wasn't in Loddiswell - it was Churchstow. He proceeded to give him directions but with the blackout and no signposts this was no easy task. He walked for what seemed hours and eventually saw a light in a field - British soldiers were there and they, with the help of a local map, sent him on his way. After walking many more miles Ken came to a farm and the farmer was just getting out of bed to go milking - it was after 5.00 a.m. but he was almost at his destination and at least a cup of tea was at hand. He did finally find his parents and although I don't think he's been back to Cranacombe since, he does know where Churchstow is!

## Jean Parnell

From the early days of 1941, British airmen and soldiers were billeted in Strete. They lived in private houses - Landcombe Cottage, Seacliff, Homelands, the Crest to name a few. Some had their wives with them. They mixed well with local people and in fact one soldier who was here with the Buffs has returned to the village almost every year since.

Warships were sometimes seen in Start Bay and occasionally 'dog fights' witnessed overhead. I remember Beesands being bombed with the loss of some lives and also raids on Dartmouth when quite a number were killed. I also remember the Focke-Wulf coming down (mentioned in my mother's, Allen Efford's and Miss Stroud's reminiscences) and a large R.A.F. lorry the next morning taking away the larger pieces of aircraft and, covered in a white sheet, what were the remains of the pilot's charred body.

Strete and the immediate area were targets for machine- gunning. On one occasion the flagpole on the church tower was split through the middle and men working in the fields had to run for cover, a couple of times.

Up to 1943, the war had not badly affected the village - we had a group of evacuees from Bristol who had returned home as it was considered safe for them to do so. During late summer, American troops began arriving in the South Hams. There was activity on the beaches with landing-craft and other vessels. The troops were welcomed into the community and were generous towards the children especially, with gifts of chocolate and sweets.

Slapton Sands was chosen geographically as the three miles of beach is similar to a stretch in Normandy between the Orne River and St. Marcouf. What was to become 'Utah' beach bore a resemblance to Slapton Ley with a freshwater lake behind and almost as a bonus, 'Omaha' beach bore a resemblance to the Strete end of the beach with its high cliffs. This therefore made an ideal assault training ground for amphibious landings being one of four major exercise areas designated for specialised use with live ammunition.

One day towards the end of my first term at Dartmouth Grammar School, I returned home to be told by my parents that we were to be evacuated. This was quite incomprehensible as others from large cities came here as evacuees - our area was thought to be fairly safe although, night after night, we could hear the drone of enemy aircraft en route for Plymouth.

Within a short time, notices were displayed advertising public meetings when all would be revealed. It was a fait accompli and people soon began preparing for their move.

Once everyone got over the incredulity of the situation, the inevitable questions arose:-

Where will we go, do we really have to leave, will the men find other work, how long might we be away?

I am still aware of the feelings of older members of the community. Many had their roots in Strete and at the age of sixty plus it would be difficult for them to settle and perhaps equally difficult for them to be accepted in other communities and environments. Despite their doubts, there was little resentment as everyone realised if this could help the War Effort it would be worth it and anyway, there was no choice, so they tried to make the best of it

I have nothing but praise for the village folk who went about their daily tasks, then tried to seek alternative work and accommodation. Each day- it was customary to see small 'knots' of people deep in discussion and no-one needed to ask the topic of the conversation.

For an eleven year old there was a slight 'restrained' excitement - new home, new school, new friends. My parents, my sister Margaret and I went to a small hamlet called Brooking, quite near Dartington. My father found work on a farm and the accommodation was a thatched cottage. I went to school in Totnes and Margaret, who was five, began school at Dartington.

Very soon U.S. troops arrived with armoured vehicles, jeeps, amphibious vehicles and tanks. The troops were under canvas and many of their vehicles and tanks were well camouflaged in nearby woods. The Americans were generous with their gifts and food to the local people.

I remember waking one night and hearing a distant rumble of what I thought was thunder, but next morning I discovered every vehicle, jeep and tank had gone and the fields were once more deserted. About two days later the news of the invasion of the Normandy coast was heard on the wireless.

We returned to Strete in January 1945 and most people had by then returned. Everyone set about clearing and cleaning and the community spirit had never been better. It was so good to see everyone again. The one thing I missed, and many others too I believe, was the row of thatched properties in the centre of the village where the King's Arms car park is situated now. Next to the village pump was the Reading/Women's Institute Room and I remember going there as a 'casualty' to be bandaged and splinted when my parents attended First Aid classes from 1940.

The Boys' Club was next with a beautifully carved overmantel, then a cottage and the blacksmith's shop on the corner. Apparently, a shell hit the thatched roof and the properties burnt down.

We all knew the trauma and upheaval had been worthwhile and even today, look upon this time with pride, having done our little bit to help the War Effort and bring an end to the war.

My father died in 1948 and my mother died in 1998. I still live in Strete and my sister Margaret in Slapton. There are now only seven people in the village who were evacuated from here.

In conclusion, I hope you may get as much enjoyment from reading this booklet as I have had in collating and writing it. Perhaps this quotation of A.P.Herbert's might be particularly relevant:-

"Somewhere in England we must write in stone
How Britain was invaded by the Yanks
And under that, a big and hearty Thanks!"